Lessons
Learned

Lessons Learned
Stories for a Working Life

Paul Farkas

IGUANA

Copyright © 2014 Paul Farkas
Published by Iguana Books
720 Bathurst Street, Suite 303
Toronto, Ontario, Canada
M5V 2R4

All rights reserved. No part of this publication may be reproduced, stored in a retrieval system or transmitted, in any form or by any means, electronic, mechanical, recording or otherwise (except brief passages for purposes of review) without the prior permission of the author or a licence from The Canadian Copyright Licensing Agency (Access Copyright). For an Access Copyright licence, visit www.accesscopyright.ca or call toll free to 1-800-893-5777.

Publisher: Greg Ioannou
Editor: Kate Unrau
Front cover image and design: Ashley James
Book layout design: Kate Unrau

Library and Archives Canada Cataloguing in Publication

Farkas, Paul, 1956-, author
        Lessons Learned : Stories for a Working Life / Paul Farkas.

 Issued in print and electronic formats.
ISBN 978-1-77180-067-9 (pbk.). ISBN 978-1-77180-068-6 (epub).
ISBN 978-1-77180-069-3 (kindle). ISBN 978-1-77180-070-9 (pdf).

        1. Work—Psychological aspects. 2. Work—Social aspects. 3. Work—life balance. 4. Success. I. Title.

BF481.F37 2014   158.7   C2014-904206-X
                                                C2014-904207-8

This is an original print edition of *Lessons Learned*.

To Elaine, Rachelle, Natalie, Jackie, Anna, and Ted.

100 times out of 100 it's my family.

Contents

Preface ix
Background xiii
1. You Don't Have to Have It All Figured Out 1
2. Your Reputation Precedes You 5
3. Communicate Your Priorities 8
4. The Importance of Humility 12
5. You Think You Know but You Don't 15
6. Learn to Forgive 19
7. Sometimes You Have to Break the Rules 22
8. Believe in Yourself 25
9. Look at the World Differently 29
10. People Are Not Simple 33
11. Loyalty Is Not Dead 37
12. You Don't Owe Your Heart 41
13. The World Isn't Entitled to Your Opinion 45
14. Don't Lie on Your Resume 48
15. Interviews Can Be Challenging 52
16. Learn to Tell a Compelling Story 56
17. Get Comfortable in Front of a Crowd 59
18. Make a List 63
19. The Complications of Culture and Language 66
20. Just Say Thanks 70
21. Reward Systems Sometimes Don't Reward 74

22. Understand Data..78
23. The Importance of Mentorship 82
24. Play to Your Strengths 86
25. Sometimes You Have to Do It Yourself.........................90
26. Sometimes You Should Trust Your Gut 93
27. Sometimes You Have to Move 97
28. We Should All Get Along (Or Not)..............................100
29. Don't Be Mean to an End 103
30. Humour is a Very Serious Thing 107
31. Fifteen Minutes of Fame 111
32. Don't Leave for Money; Don't Stay Out of Fear.......115
33. The Power of Money..120
34. Find and Keep the Right Partner................................124
35. Find Your Reason 128
36. Tell Me a Story 133

Preface

In the summer of 2013, our youngest daughter, Jackie, was about to enter university. Late one August evening she was very anxious about her new adventure, primarily because she didn't yet have her life path figured out. Apparently, "all" of her friends did.

Her mother and I sat down with her for something of an intervention. We told her lots of stories about our past experiences and that what she was feeling was not all that different from what we had been through. Our tête-a-tête-a-tête seemed to work. Two weeks later, Jackie was in the midst of freshman orientation at Laurier University, and she hasn't looked back.

Unbeknownst to us at the time, Jackie's sister Natalie was listening from the other side of the door. Afterwards she pulled me aside and said that she would remember our talk with Jackie as a great example of parenting, if and when she had kids. A compliment from my daughter about parenting skills — where had this come from?

Mark Twain once wrote: "When I was a boy of fourteen, my father was so ignorant I could hardly stand to have the old man around. But when I got to be twenty-one, I was astonished by how much he'd learned in seven years."

As I write this, my "kids" are 23, 21, and 18, still in school, and about to embark on their careers. I have about thirty years of experience, primarily in the area of Human Resources, and I figure now is the time to provide them with my advice about the work environment before Natalie and her sisters revert to believing I am an old ignoramus.

Two books written about 25 years ago by G. Kingsley Ward, entitled *Letters of a Businessman to His Son* and *Letters of a Businessman to His Daughter,* provided advice about Ward's experiences in the world of business. Though his original audience is clear, he obviously published these for a broader readership. I enjoyed those "letters" and took away some valuable lessons, and I wanted to do the same thing for my kids — and perhaps a broader audience — from a Human Resources perspective.

But I didn't want to provide advice to them in the form of a "how-to." An old proverb states: "Tell me and I'll forget; show me and I may remember; involve me and I'll understand."

Stories involve the listener, and illustrating points with stories is, I believe, the best way to ensure that learning and understanding take hold. In fact, I believe that the ability to tell a compelling story is essential, especially in leadership positions. (See Chapter 16, "Learn to Tell a Compelling Story.")

One of the techniques I have used routinely when interviewing potential managers was to ask them to "tell a story that illustrates a point." While there are many criteria to determine the successful candidate in a recruitment effort, the on-point and compelling stories I heard during these interviews were often great predictors of a candidate's success in a leadership role.

As interesting as my stories may be to my kids, I realize that to provide value to a broader audience, stories told by the reader or the reader's parent, mentor, or counsellor might be more relevant in illustrating similar points. For that reason, I have included a chapter at the end of this book that provides a series of behavioural-based questions to assist in the development of such narratives. My thought is that by using my stories as examples and the questions as guides, the reader will have access to lessons that resonate on a more personal level.

My thirty years of experience come with thirty years of stories. In the following pages, you'll find some of my favourites. They all happened, and they're all true — at least my recollection of them is true.

I have changed some of the names and locations to "protect the innocent," as the old detective stories might say. But in actuality, it was more to protect those who asked not to be named or who might be more apt to look unfavourably on my inclusion of them. At the end of the day, however, we are all just characters in each others' stories.

And for those who might be upset by my telling of these, please read my chapter on forgiveness. (See Chapter 6.)

I found the compilation of these stories to be both an entertaining and a valuable experience. I hope that you find the same in reading them.

Background

In order to put the stories on the following pages into perspective, below is a brief summary of my background.

I grew up as the only child of a middle-class family in suburban Montreal. My parents, Anna and Ted Farkas, both worked outside of the home — my mother as a speech therapist and my father as a purchasing agent.

I attended school in Montreal, leading to a degree in biochemistry from McGill University. After graduation, I attended the Business School at the University of Western Ontario and received a Master of Business Administration.

My career began in Western Canada although the majority of my work experience has been obtained in and around the Toronto area.

I have held a number of positions — mostly Human Resources–related — in a variety of industries: newspaper (*Calgary Herald*), engineering and construction (Delta Projects and Stone & Webster), oil and gas (PetroCanada Products), food processing (National Cheese), automotive (Hyundai — twice), and consulting (TGO Consulting).

I am surrounded by women. My wife of close to 30 years, Elaine, conducts clinical research in the pharmaceutical industry. We have three daughters — Rachelle, Natalie, and Jacqueline (Jackie). Even our cat Monty is female.

My children, although born in Toronto, have been raised properly. When we attend hockey games, it is always in the *bleu, blanc, et rouge* of our beloved Montreal Canadiens.

1. You Don't Have to Have It All Figured Out

When planning for a year, plant corn. When planning for a decade, plant trees. When planning for life, train and educate people.

Chinese Proverb

Anna Farkas was a speech therapist — and a pioneer for her time. She received a master's degree in the 1950s, when it was still unusual for women to have any university education. As a therapist, she worked in a variety of settings, but for most of my childhood she spent her time working in one hospital or another. I would often visit my mom at work, even occasionally helping her to perform audiology exams on her patients. As a result, I became accustomed to the hospital environment, and when I considered where my career might start, the medical profession seemed like a logical choice.

In college, I concentrated my studies in health sciences and decided to enrol in the biochemistry program at McGill, thinking that it would be my best bet to get into medicine. A few days before my classes started, I met with my academic advisor, a professor in the biochem department. He asked me what I wanted to be "when I grew up," and I told him I was going to be a doctor.

He said: "No you're not."

And when I asked why not, he said, "Well, to be truthful I don't know. But statistically, two-thirds of the people who enter the biochemistry program who think they want to be doctors end up doing something else. I suggest you have a plan B in mind. What's your plan B?"

I told him I didn't have one.

"Well here's a thought," he said. "Go get an MBA and make yourself indispensible to the pharmaceutical industry."

I did get an MBA in the end, but I still haven't worked for a pharmaceutical firm, and at this point likely never will. I didn't have it figured out then — and to be truthful, I'm not sure I ever got it figured out. And I'm not all that certain many people do, even if they've been working in their fields for a long time.

Shortly after we were married, Elaine and I had the opportunity to vacation with the Rucker family. I played baseball with Brian Rucker when I first moved to Toronto, and he and his wife, Cheryl, had subsequently moved out west to join a law firm in downtown Calgary. Brian was very smart, quick witted, and funny as hell. On the surface, he seemed to have it all.

Early one morning as the sun was rising, I went out onto the porch of the lodge that our two families had rented for the week in the Rocky Mountains. I thought I would be alone, but Brian was there staring out at the idyllic scene. The ice caps glimmered in the distance and the morning sun shimmered off the lake. I had no idea how long he had been there, but I assumed a position at the other end of the porch so as not to interrupt his seeming trance-like relaxation. And then he broke the silence.

"You know, I'm basically a prostitute," he said.

"What?" I asked.

He said again, "I'm a prostitute. I can take one side of an argument and argue it convincingly. I can take the other side and argue it just as convincingly. It just depends who pays me. Sometimes I hate what I do, but I can't get out."

Well, this blew me away. I had assumed he loved his work and the lifestyle that it brought, and I'm sure that oftentimes he did. But the level of dissatisfaction he had expressed about his job threw me. I thought he had it all figured out.

Several years later, I was recruiting to fill a corporate counsel position. The eventual successful candidate was Heather Hart. In our initial interview, I had asked why she would want to leave her downtown firm to come and work for us. I forget what she actually said, but it was an appropriate response and everyone in the room bought it. Heather was one of the sharpest corporate lawyers I have come across — she took her job seriously, but not herself. We would talk fairly regularly about lots of things — work-related and otherwise.

One day I asked her why she really left her firm to join us. She told me that she was on the verge of becoming a partner in the firm, one of their youngest ever. But she looked at the partners — many who had been doing their jobs for twenty years or more — and said to herself that wasn't the life she wanted to live. And unlike Brian, she chose to get out before the "golden handcuffs" were on. Heather is still in law for now, but not working at what she thought she'd be doing when she used to imagine it back when she was in school.

In fact as it turns out, many people don't end up doing what they originally envisioned — even those who pursue specific career-focused programs like law. The statistics show that upward of one-third of law school graduates in Canada are doing something other than practising law five years after graduation.

I have had eight jobs over the course of my career, most of them Human Resources related. There is no way I would have predicted that while I was studying biochemistry.

So here's what I learned: Resist the urge to think that you should have your path figured out by the time you're in university or even thereafter. Over the course of your career, you will very likely work for many employers (yourself included) and in many industries — even some employers and some industries that don't yet exist.

You may think that some of your friends have it all figured out. Some may — but most don't. And even those who think they do will be surprised how their careers unfold in the end.

A career plan is fine, but if it doesn't work out as you expected, don't panic. Continue to learn and acquire new skills that will help you to find a role that you'll be happy with and where you believe you can make a meaningful contribution. Be open to a plan B. Or a plan C or D.

2. Your Reputation Precedes You

It takes many good deeds to build a good reputation, and only one bad one to lose it.

Benjamin Franklin

Ted Farkas was a purchasing agent for all of his professional life, first for a furniture manufacturer and then for the Alberta government. As a buyer, my dad would at times be subject to certain incentives to acquire a product or a service on behalf of a vendor. When I was a kid, he would tell me that he had a common response whenever he was offered a bribe. He would accept the item or article, consider it, and then pass it back saying, "Sorry. It's not enough."

He would then suggest a ridiculous amount of money that he would need in order to accept. When came the inevitable reply, "You're crazy," my dad would say, "Look, I'm human. I have my price. But if I'm going to corrupt my values, that's what it's going to cost you."

According to my dad, no vendor ever made a second offer.

When I worked at Hyundai initially, the President sent me to Korea to learn about Korean culture and to experience the country and its people. A number of our managers had previously made the trip, and I asked a few of them what to expect.

Lessons Learned

Lloyd Brummund was the head of the Service group at the time. I had gotten to know Lloyd a little bit — we played tennis a few times after work and he usually kicked my butt. But I didn't know him well enough that I could always decipher whether he was telling me the truth or having a little fun with the "new guy." I was in his office a couple of days before I left and I told him about my pending trip.

"Be very careful," he told me. "Your hosts will try to get you drunk. They'll be testing you. Your reputation will get back to Canada before you will."

That afternoon, the itinerary for my trip arrived. Hyundai was very organized, and every aspect of a meeting or a trip had been carefully planned out in detail. I looked at the agenda, which included social activities, and there seemed to be absolutely no opportunity for the kind of "trouble" that Lloyd had suggested. I assumed it was one of his jokes.

I arrived in Seoul on a Sunday morning and was to leave the following Friday evening. A Korean manager of roughly my age was assigned to provide me with a personalized tour. He took me around the head office, and then we drove off into the countryside to view other Hyundai facilities and Korean cultural and historic sites. We talked about Korean life and philosophies, and I told him about my experiences in Canada. Every visit at every place was timed to coincide with the agenda that had been provided.

We arrived back in Seoul on Thursday afternoon with just enough time to freshen up before a scheduled dinner with an ex-President of Hyundai Auto Canada — the man who had hired me, but for whom I had never worked. He was noted for being a teetotaller, so I knew that there would be no alcohol on this last night of my trip. And I was scheduled to attend a meeting back at head office very early Friday morning. I knew Lloyd was full of it.

My "tour guide manager" picked me up at the hotel at 5:30 and informed me that, with much regret, my host had to cancel our dinner. Instead, we would be going out with his senior manager and some co-workers. The hair on the back of my neck started to stand up.

That night we attended a restaurant and two bars before our last stop at a local "geisha house." There was a lot of booze. There was a lot of opportunity to get into a lot of trouble. And, I *was* being tested.

So here's what I learned: There's nothing more important than your reputation. And life will test it regularly. These tests may be overt — like my evening in Korea — or more discrete, in day-to-day situations. Never assume you know how you'll behave before you are put into a situation. You are human; you have a price. Just remember that whatever you do, your behaviour will be judged and your reputation will get home before you do. Make sure your price is worth it.

3. Communicate Your Priorities

If you don't stand for something, you will fall for anything.

Attributed to Martin Luther King Jr.

Everyone has heard the story of the guy who starts his career in the mailroom and moves up to the top position. Most of us assume that the story is a fairy tale — like *Sleeping Beauty*, or like the Toronto Maple Leafs one day winning the Stanley Cup again. But I know this story to be true. I've worked for that guy.

Ed Dorr was the President of Stone & Webster Canada during my tenure with the company and my boss for about five years. Ed was unpretentious, practical, and a little gruff — characteristics that made complete sense given his background. A native of Holland, he came to Canada penniless and began his career, literally, in the mailroom of a construction company.

When I was originally brought on at Stone & Webster, the company had formed a hiring committee comprising the senior management group as well as the external recruiter assigned to the search. At the time, Ed was Stone & Webster's Vice President of Construction and, as such, was a member of the committee. But during my initial interview, Ed was overseeing construction at one of the company sites in Northern Ontario and couldn't attend. For years he would joke that the only reason I was hired in the first place was that he was not present at my interview — at least I think he was joking.

Ed had taken over the role of VP Construction from a predecessor well into his seventies who had been made Special Assistant to the President. Ed and the former VP didn't exactly see eye-to-eye on many issues, and over time they'd had a few corporate battles. As the financial situation of the parent company in Boston worsened, the company decided it didn't need a septuagenarian Assistant to the President as an added expense, so the company decided to retire him. Either as a practical joke or as a means of keeping expenses down, the President put Ed Dorr in charge of planning the retirement party. Ed was not happy about this assignment, but his boss insisted.

All of the senior management and their spouses were expected to attend the gathering. But due to the company's poor financial situation, only drinks would be covered — not the cost of the meals. No one was impressed with the situation, and on the night of the soiree, the attendees made all attempts to get their money's worth.

Elaine was about eight months pregnant with our second daughter, Natalie, at the time. She hadn't had a drink throughout the pregnancy, but on that evening, late in the third trimester, she said, "what the heck." Not wanting to overdo it, she decided one drink would be enough; but not wanting to feel left out either, she ordered the most expensive drink on the menu, a Kir Royale — a mixture of champagne and crème de cassis.

A couple of weeks later, I found myself in Ed Dorr's office as his secretary brought in the mail — including the invoice for the drinks from the retirement party. Ed opened the invoice and immediately blanched. He thundered: "Look at these lushes. Look how much they drank. Look at the size of this bill. And ... some asshole even had the audacity to order a Kir Royale."

As if I had been waiting to use the line for years, I calmly said, "Ed, that was no asshole; that was my wife." Then I explained what had happened. Seeing that flummoxed look on his face was priceless.

But my most memorable meeting with Ed was the first time we got together in his office. Because he had missed my initial session with the hiring committee, he called me in shortly after I joined to "get to know me." I was sitting across the same desk from which he would later refer to my wife as an asshole. After some small talk, he leaned across and said: "Your career or your family: what do you choose?"

"Pardon?" I said.

He repeated, "Your career or your family. What do you choose?"

I realized what he was getting at, so I started to dance. "You know, Ed, both are important to me. It depends on the situation. Sometimes you have to put the job first, sometimes family considerations come first."

He slammed his fist into the desk and shouted: "Don't boooolshit me!" That's actually how it came out with his Dutch accent. "Your career or your family. What do you choose?"

I looked him in the eye and said, "Ed, one hundred times out of one hundred, my family."

He leaned back and said in a soft voice, "Thank you for your honesty."

Several years later and after Ed Dorr became President, Elaine faced what might have been a serious medical condition. While we were fortunate that everything turned out well, there was a period of about two months when we weren't sure — and it was hell. When I told Ed what was going on, he said to me, "You take as much time as you need to. One hundred times out of one hundred, it's your family."

I never worked for a boss I respected more.

So here's what I learned: At some point in your career you will have to make a decision about your priorities. No one can tell you what they should be — you have to figure them out for yourself. And once you do, you have to stay true to them. And if you're ever asked where your priorities are, be honest. If they don't like your answer, you're in the wrong place.

4. The Importance of Humility

If you are filled with pride, then you will have no room for wisdom.

African proverb

As an undergraduate, I attended McGill University and received a Bachelor of Science in biochemistry. Of course, McGill was, and still is, the best science school in Canada — unbiased opinion of course. Go McGill!

I had hoped to attend medical school after graduation, but my interests shifted, and to be honest my marks and MCAT scores (the exams required for entry to med school) also indicated otherwise. I took the GMAT exams — the exams required for graduate studies in business — one week after having written the MCATs. The difficulty I had writing the MCATs was inversely proportional to the ease I found taking the GMATs, and the results reflected the same. So I applied to business school.

In those days, unlike today, it was fairly common for a student to attend business school immediately after undergrad without any significant work experience. So it wasn't particularly unusual that I was accepted to the business school at the University of Western Ontario — now known as Ivey, but then known as the Western

School of Business. Of course Western was, and still is, the best business school in Canada — unbiased opinion of course. Go Western!

After graduation, I made my way out to Alberta, which was booming at the time. Eastern Canada was mired in a recession and I thought it would be easier to start my career in the west.

My second job out of school was at a consulting engineering firm — Delta Projects in Calgary. Calgary was the centre of the oil and gas industry in Canada, and Delta was primarily involved in providing services to that sector. Specifically, Delta specialized in the conversion of sulphur-infused gas (sour gas) into desulphinated gas (sweet gas), which could be used commercially. They held a number of patents for the desulphination process, all using a form of membrane technology. And the majority of these patents belonged to Robert Silverman, who held a PhD in process chemistry.

Dr. Silverman was originally from California but had moved up to Calgary to pursue his career. He met an Alberta girl, fell in love with both her and the city of Calgary, and the rest — as they say — was history. Silverman was an acknowledged expert in the field of membrane technology and was routinely sought out to speak at conferences and symposia throughout North America. We live in a time when the word "genius" is thrown about very loosely, but Bob Silverman was a genius.

I joined Delta as a Human Resources Representative, initially responsible for the recruitment of staff. I had been introduced to Bob when I first joined the company. I found him very pleasant but, like me, quite shy, so our interactions were limited.

One day, I was sitting in my office. There was a knock on the door and I looked up. If I am totally honest, I probably looked to the side. My office overlooked the Rocky Mountains and I would routinely stare out the window and marvel at the beauty surrounding me. (From a real-estate perspective, my career never quite reached that lofty height again — from a windowless office outside the production floor of a cheese factory to a building overlooking uptown Toronto, and other locations with views to various parking lots.) In any case, the person at my door was Bob Silverman. I had assumed that he wanted to discuss the recruitment of a new grad for his process engineering group, but I was wrong — he surprised me.

Bob asked if it was true that I had a degree in biochemistry. I told him that I did. He asked if I had studied membranes and I told him that, yes, I had. He then said that he had a particularly difficult problem he was unable to solve. He had discussed it with his group and they couldn't come up with an answer. He thought that before he went outside the organization he'd ask if I might be able to help. I said I would try, and he outlined the problem.

I would love to tell you that I had the answer. I didn't, and I told him so. But Bob Silverman taught me a lesson that day that has stayed with me for the remainder of my career.

Here was an acknowledged expert in his field, a true genius. He had a problem. And whom did he come to for help? A fresh-faced kid less than a year out of school — in the Human Resources Department of all places. Because he thought I might be able to help him.

In Silverman's world there were no barriers to learning, no hierarchy, no ego. If he thought someone could help him to solve a problem, he would ask.

I didn't solve his problem. But from that day until I left the company, we had many discussions about science and about life, and he was always as free with his advice as he was asking for it.

So here's what I learned: Don't ever stop learning or think you know it all. Never imagine that you're above asking someone else — anyone else — if they might be able to help you solve a problem. Understand that one of the measures of true genius is humility.

Never let your ego get so big that you won't ask for help.

5. You Think You Know but You Don't

If we could read the secret history of our enemies, we should find in each man's life sorrow and suffering enough to disarm all hostility.

Henry Wadsworth Longfellow

Every now and then, there will be a piece on the news about some crackpot who shoots up a school, his ex-workplace, or some other location where innocent people are killed. The media will subsequently interview a neighbour who expresses shock: "He was such a nice, quiet person. I never would have suspected he would do anything like that."

And if you're like me, often your initial reaction is, "Oh, please. Only an idiot wouldn't have seen the signs."

My first job out of school was at the *Calgary Herald*, the local newspaper. I worked in the Human Resources Department and our offices were next door to Advertising. The building was such that we shared a common elevator, but both departments were behind separate closed doors. I knew most of the people in Advertising by name and we would chat to and from trips to the coffee machine.

One Friday afternoon I was leaving work and waiting for the elevator. One of the commercial artists from Advertising appeared

Lessons Learned

and stood next to me. I knew him to exchange small talk and thought he was a really nice guy. We began to chat about our plans for the weekend. He asked whether I was married and I said no. He said, "Yeah, you're lucky," and we shared a knowing little laugh about the benefits of single life.

I woke up the next morning to the news that he had gone home and murdered his wife. Had I been interviewed the next day, I would have said, "He was such a nice, quiet person. I never would have suspected he would do anything like that." I would have been one of those idiots.

We think we know another person, but we really don't.

I once had a professor at school who said that every one of us looks for two things from other people: 1) we want people to like us, and 2) we want people to *be* like us. After leaving school and with the hindsight of working with a wide variety of people over many years, I'm not sure about the first statement. For some people, it's nice when others like us; for others, it doesn't make much of a difference. Everyone's needs are different. I think my professor needed to be liked and therefore assumed that all people needed the same.

Nonetheless, I would add one point to his argument ... 3) we not only want people to *be* like us, but we *assume* that everyone is just like us. It's a very bad assumption.

Someone once explained to me the derivation of the word "understand." He used the story of a child watching a parade from the back of a crowd standing on his father's shoulders. The father couldn't see what was happening, so the child described what he saw. The father literally was standing under his son, and he saw the world through his son's eyes.

I thought this was a neat story. Alas, I looked up the origin of the word "understand" only to find out that it was unknown. But, given that wordsmiths don't know how the word derived, I still use the image of the father and son as the true meaning of "understanding," that is to say, seeing the world through the eyes of another person.

Over the course of my career, I have been exposed to a number of different personality-profiling tools. All of them point to the very different ways that each of us interacts with the world around him. Some of us like the energy of crowds; some of us are energized by being alone. Some of us revere authority; others can't stand it. The list of ways that we differ is endless — yet we all have to work and live together.

Chris Argyris is an often-quoted educator who coined the term, "Ladder of Inference." We climb the ladder by observing the behaviour of another person and attributing their behaviour to our view of the world. We reach the top of the ladder when we take actions based on our assumptions, to the detriment of our relationship with the person we observe. We don't realize that other people may behave differently than we would simply because their views of the world differ from ours.

One day I walked into the office of one of our managers. I knew he had been under considerable stress because of his workload, and he had a reputation for being very abrasive at the best of times. But I had been waiting on him to review something for me; I was under a tight deadline myself, and he was holding up the process. When I asked for his feedback, he lit into me. I assumed it was his normal personality coming through in combination with the stress of work, so I purposefully didn't react. But internally I climbed the ladder — I thought, *what an asshole.*

Fortunately before I reached the top rung, I asked him what the problem was. He told me that he had just received a phone call from home. A close family member had just died. Obviously I'd had no idea, but that information put the entire interaction under a very different light.

We often attribute behavioural differences to malicious intent, when in fact our interpretation is based on a failure to understand where the other person is coming from.

Lessons Learned

So here's what I learned: Over the course of your career you're going to work with people who have a wide variety of personalities, differing views of the world, and many things on their personal plates. Oftentimes people will behave in a manner that you don't understand and that drives you crazy. Don't climb the ladder of inference and assume that their behaviours are intended to piss you off. Attempt to find out where they're coming from by inquiring why they behaved the way they did, and try to truly understand them — see the world through their eyes.

Don't assume you know another person. You don't.

6. Learn to Forgive

People can be more forgiving than you can imagine. But you have to forgive yourself. Let go of what's bitter and move on.

Bill Cosby

John MacDonald was the head of Human Resources for a rival engineering firm at the time that I was at Stone & Webster. We were competitors and friends at the same time. I had a lot of respect for John's ability — he was from the Maritimes and had that simple yet wise way of looking at and commenting on the world. He would "cut to the chase," and most often what he would say was bang on target.

I had become the President of our industry group — the Engineering Human Resources Association of Canada — and John had been elected Vice President. Every year, the association would hold an annual conference of engineering Human Resources leaders in one of our three regions — Quebec, Ontario, and the West. We would rotate the locations so as to keep the meetings fresh and to spread the workload around — organizing the annual conference could be quite time consuming. This time it was our turn.

John was also the head of the Ontario region, and as such he was in charge of our efforts to organize the conference. As the President of the association as well as a local Ontario chapter member, I would work closely with him in the organizing effort.

About ten months before the event, the Ontario chapter got together to determine responsibilities and lay out the budget and timetable for the conference. Unfortunately, Stone & Webster was just at the beginning of a market downturn in which we would lose projects and, as a result, some very good people. John's firm had the opposite "problem" — they were growing fast and needed resources. The previous week, they had poached one of our best and most senior engineers. John and I hadn't talked since the resignation was announced, and as we entered the meeting room, there was a bit of unspoken tension between us.

As the meeting started, there were a couple of new faces in the group of 15 or so. John asked the participants to introduce themselves around the table. After the first new group member gave her intro, John welcomed her to the Association.

"I think you'll find we are a pretty unique group," he said. "I consider some of these people my closest colleagues and resources for knowledge, yet at the same time we are trying to kill each other and steal each other's staff."

At this I immediately shouted: "Yeah, FUCK YOU, John!"

The room went silent. But John, who was sitting next to me, burst out laughing and slapped me on the back. And at this, the rest of the room cracked up — with the exception of our new colleague, who seemed slightly confused. After the meeting I apologized to John for what I had said, and the tension between us was broken.

Now, had I thought about it a little more clearly, would I have said what I did? Probably not. It wasn't exactly the most professional thing I've done in my career. In fact you might argue that it was pretty stupid. But we all say and do pretty stupid things at times. We all say and do pretty insensitive things as well. And hurtful things. We all say and do these things because we're human, and humans make mistakes.

But there's a fundamental difference between malice and mistake: Had I used the language I did with a different intent, or to a different person who I knew was likely to be offended, then I would have crossed the line. And had I continued to do or say something that another person told me was offensive to him, then I also would have crossed that line. In this case I simply made a mistake ... and I didn't do it again.

So here's what I learned: Over the course of your career (and your life in general) you will say and do some pretty stupid, hurtful, and insensitive things. Congratulations, you're human.

Many people tend to live in the past with regrets about what they've said or done. Don't be one of them. Apologize, ask for forgiveness, and move on — and don't do it again.

Many people tend to live in the past with grudges about what others have said or done to them. Don't be one of them either. If you're on the receiving end of stupid, hurtful, and insensitive behaviour or language, speak up. Pull the individual aside and tell them their behaviour or language is inappropriate and you want it to stop. If they apologize, accept the apology and forgive. If not, and if the behaviour persists even though you've put them on notice, then you have the right to claim their actions represent something more sinister.

Learn to forgive yourself and learn to forgive others. Forgiveness will go a long way to your ultimate success and to your own happiness.

7. Sometimes You Have to Break the Rules

To raise new questions, new possibilities, to regard old problems from a new angle, requires a creative imagination and marks the real advances in science.

Albert Einstein

I worked as the head of Human Resources for Stone & Webster Canada for close to 15 years. In the 1980s, Stone & Webster Inc., our parent company based out of Boston, had made a number of bad gambles relating to the construction of nuclear power plants and began to experience financial problems from which it would ultimately not recover. In the late 1990s the company filed for Chapter 11 bankruptcy protection. The Canadian subsidiary, however, never went bankrupt. During one stretch, Stone & Webster Canada was experiencing a major boom in project work at the time that our parent was in distress. During this period, Boston had instituted a company-wide salary freeze across all subsidiaries, including Canada.

One Friday afternoon during this period, one of our Chief Engineers came into my office and said he had a big problem. He had an engineer who had just been made an offer by our main competitor,

SNC, that would include a 20 percent increase in his pay. The engineer was working on a critical phase of one of our projects, but he told the Chief Engineer that while he understood the sensitivity of leaving during that point in the project, for family reasons, 20 percent was too much for him to turn down. Further, as the parent company was in difficulty, he could see the "writing on the wall" for the Canadian operation. He gave his boss until the following Monday to let him know if he could match the offer.

The Chief Engineer said that this employee was crucial to the success of the project and he had to keep him until its completion. He knew about the salary freeze and asked what we could do about it. I told him officially there was nothing we could do — Boston was tracking all salary changes and there would be no exceptions. We both stared at our shoes for a few minutes considering our options. Finally, I knew what we would do. We were going to fire him.

The Chief Engineer suggested that I was losing it and that I didn't fully understand the situation. I assured him that I did. I said that I knew that Boston was tracking all changes to salary, but they had not yet instituted a hiring freeze. They were still allowing subsidiaries to hire in order to meet the needs of projects. I also knew that they weren't monitoring starting salaries. So I suggested that we should "fire" his engineer on Friday — in our HR system — and "re-hire" him on Monday with a 20 percent salary increase. We certainly wouldn't tell the engineer he was fired, and no one would be the wiser — no one other than the Chief Engineer and me, that is.

It worked. The engineer stayed. He subsequently left for SNC, but only after his work on the project was completed. And Boston never learned what we had done.

Organizations put new rules or policies in place to address a certain issue at the time they are implemented. Most times these policies continue to make sense. But occasionally situations change or the intent behind the rule is obscured by time. When this occurs, the organization's policy can actually negatively affect its ability to succeed in whatever its mission is.

One of the questions I typically ask a prospective candidate when I am recruiting, especially for positions at a more senior level, is "however you define it, give me an example of a time when you broke the rules." I typically give the candidate a long time to collect his or her thoughts and think about an answer.

The reason I ask the question is two-fold. First, most senior-level people have come across this organizational dilemma in the past. I want to know whether the candidates have the ability to come up with creative solutions to an organization's own roadblocks. But second, and more importantly, I want to know if the solutions they come up with cross any moral, ethical, or legal boundaries. And the answers to this question have been surprising.

Some people have come up with examples that were trivial or said that they had never broken any rules. In my view, these people were either lying, uncreative, or unable to think quickly enough to handle the question. Those people were down-graded. Others came up with examples that clearly crossed ethical and even legal boundaries. Those people were eliminated.

So here's what I learned: Not all rules are created equal. By my definition, "breaking the rules" involves thinking out of the box to come up with a creative solution to an organization's self-imposed problem. Sometimes in your career, you'll have to break the rules. Only you will be able to figure out when you must take that step. But when you do, always ensure that your actions meet three criteria: 1) You must never break the law; 2) you must never do anything immoral; and 3) you must never do anything unethical.

8. Believe in Yourself

Trust yourself. You know more than you think you do.

Dr. Benjamin Spock

When I was in the MBA program at Western, I really didn't know the direction I wanted my career to go. I had completed my undergraduate degree in biochemistry at McGill, and by the end of those studies, I was pretty sure science wasn't for me. I actually enjoyed the psychology and sociology courses I had taken as electives more than the core science courses I had to take to earn my degree. I thought that if there were a way to make money in those areas, I might want to pursue it, but I didn't yet know how. When I was introduced to the field of organizational behaviour as part of the MBA program, I thought maybe I'd found it. I took as many courses in that area as possible, and that interest led me to a career in Human Resources.

My first job out of school was as a Recruitment Specialist with the *Calgary Herald*. It was a tremendous break as I didn't have any HR experience. Looking back, I didn't even know all that much about the job other than the theories I had learned in school. But the Human Resources Manager saw something he liked and hired me anyway. My function was primarily recruiting, and I attended night classes to learn how to interview, never having done it before.

After about nine months in the job, I started to get bored doing nothing but interviewing candidates for the many openings the newspaper had. My colleague Annette worked on other kinds of projects in the same department, and she helped me to understand the sorts of things she was working on. Annette's friend, David Watson, was the head of HR for Delta Projects, an engineering company, and he was looking for an assistant. When Annette told him about me, and about how I was becoming restless at the *Herald*, he asked me to come in and interview. Annette must have really promoted me: The interview lasted an hour, and David talked about the company, his vision of HR, and his experiences, among other things, for about 55 minutes. The next day he offered me the job.

I panicked. I realized that all of my Human Resources experience was in recruiting and interviewing, and I knew nothing about most of the other areas he'd need me for. I turned the job down. When Annette found out, she was livid. She called me an idiot (or something to that effect) and said that I had far more capability than I gave myself credit for. She told me to call David back and accept. And bolstered by nothing more than her belief in me, I did. David threw the full gamut of the HR functions at me, encouraged me to try my best, and when I got stuck, he helped me to understand what I was doing. To this day, I consider David my mentor.

Many years later, I started work at another company as the head of the Human Resources department. On my first day there, a Monday, I inherited a team from my predecessor, who had been terminated the previous Friday. I had no idea what to expect — whether the staff's loyalties would lie with the person who had brought them together or with the "new guy." It was a real possibility that by Tuesday I would be faced with an open revolt and no staff. But fortunately they stayed.

We were a group of four initially. There was lots of work to do, and unless we changed the way that the department functioned, with such a small group, we were going to fail.

One of the mandates that had been given to me by our President was to put a system in place that would allow us to address the wide range of data requests required of us. He also wanted a general cleanup of the department processes, which he deemed to be ineffective. The only way I could see us doing all of these tasks, and our day-to-day jobs at the same time, was through better use of technology. I had built HR systems previously and wanted to do the same at this company — bringing together the pieces that everyone was working on separately into a common framework.

On the first morning I assembled the group, I told them that if they wanted to leave, I would understand perfectly, but that if they wanted to stay, here was the vision: We would build the most efficient and effective department in the industry. We weren't going to get any more people to help — we were it. It was up to the four of us to meet the challenge.

One of the group had used Microsoft Access to a limited extent in the past — that was the database tool I wanted to use to build our system. The others hadn't, but they were both very technically competent in the use of other systems and keen to learn. As the system developed, at one point or another each one of them expressed some doubt about their ability to accomplish their pieces of the puzzle. Each time, I expressed my confidence in them — as both David and Annette had done for me years earlier — and when there was an issue that someone couldn't handle, we worked on it together.

The system started to take shape after about a month of work, and we continued to improve it for the five years that I stayed with the company.

About two years into the development, the Facilities Department was moved to the Human Resources group. This department comprised four people responsible for keeping the building running and administering the large volume of the company's internal vehicle fleet. When I started to look at their processes, I realized that their systems were primarily manual. What I didn't realize was that the department head was trained as an engineer. He was at least as proficient in the use of Access as the rest of us, but no one had ever asked him to automate his processes.

I gave him the same speech about efficiency and effectiveness, and I challenged him to have his team become the best Facilities group in the industry. He accepted the challenge and would often work on weekends developing components that would automate previously manual processes. He not only developed systems that no one else in the industry had, but he became a resource for the rest of us as we continued to improve the HR system.

So here's what I learned: As you progress in your career, you will be asked to meet new challenges that, at first blush, might seem intimidatingly beyond your scope. You will be asked to do those things because someone believes that you can — *and you can*. Don't shy away from these opportunities out of fear. We all have reserves that we don't realize are available to us. On the other hand, don't be afraid to ask for the help that you need in order to achieve your tasks.

And when you get into positions where you rely on others, remember that people often have latent talents that you don't know about. Draw those talents out, develop them, encourage them, and use them effectively.

9. Look at the World Differently

If you don't like something, change it. If you can't change it, change your attitude. Don't complain.

Maya Angelou

Back in elementary school, I was very good at arithmetic — top of the class. I could add, subtract, multiply, and divide faster and more accurately than anyone else. Arithmetic is essentially linear; it occurs along *the* x axis in a straight line on a graph. When you add or multiply, the operation moves toward the right on the axis. When you subtract or divide, it moves to the left. It's pretty simple stuff.

Then I went to high school. There, another dimension was added to the study of mathematics — the y axis. The second dimension allowed for the study of geometry, algebra, and the like. I was really good in math in high school as well. Not always at the top of the class, but pretty close, and my math marks were among my highest in high school.

Then I attended university. I was introduced to advanced algebra, calculus, and differential equations. And again I remained at or near the top of my classes ... until Calculus III.

In Calculus III, a third dimension was added to the mix — the z axis. "In theory," said my professor, "the z axis is a line away from the page, in a direction pointing straight toward you." But I had a problem. No matter how I tried, I couldn't visualize the z axis in my mind. And as my learning style was, and continues to be, very visual, I had to be able to *see* something to understand it.

I worked harder on Calculus III than I ever had in any math course up to that point. I memorized all of the formulae. I read and then re-read the math text. I struggled through all the assignments. But I wasn't getting it, and I knew it.

Half way through the semester, I wrote the mid-term. The advice that most experts give on how to successfully write an exam is to read through all the questions and solve the problems you know first. I did just that. But when I came to the end and hadn't written anything on my paper, I knew I was in real trouble. I went back to the beginning and cobbled together answers to each of the questions, with the full knowledge that I had no clue what I was doing.

We wrote on a Tuesday and received the results the following Friday. Magically, I earned a grade of 40 percent, but last I knew, 40 percent was still a flunk. It was the first and only time in my life that I failed a math exam.

I was devastated. After class I wandered aimlessly through downtown Montreal until it was time to go home. I found myself at Windsor Station, the main train terminal. Normally I would have taken the Metro home, but there would be a suburban train leaving shortly and I decided to take that instead. I wanted to change up my routine.

While waiting for the train, I ran into a buddy of mine — Jerry Molnar. Jerry was an engineering student at McGill and had taken Calculus III the year before. He looked at me and said, "What's with you? You look like your dog just died." I told him that I had just flunked the Calc III midterm.

"That's unusual," he replied. "You're good at math, I thought. What's the problem?"

I told him about my inability to picture the z axis. He said, "That's easy. Just picture it coming straight out of the page at you."

I "thanked" him for his insight but told him that was exactly what I couldn't visualize.

By this time we were on the train. "Look in the corner," he said. "There's the x axis, there's the y axis, there's the z axis."

When I turned to inspect the corner, there it was as clear as day: The y axis came down vertically, and the z axis and x axis were at 90 degrees to each other in an inverted V shape. I had never looked at it like that before.

When I got home, I immediately opened my last assignment. Everything clicked. Like magic, all of the memorization I had done made complete sense. I could now visualize what was going on in Calculus III.

The following Tuesday, I arrived for class about 15 minutes early, alone except for the professor, who was completing a fairly complicated equation on the white board at the front of the classroom. It was like one of the equations you see in Sheldon and Leonard's apartment on *The Big Bang Theory*. I looked at the equation, and an error in the last argument of the second line jumped out at me. I called out from my seat, "I think there's a mistake on line two."

The professor turned around and looked at me with an expression that said *who are you?* Not surprising, since I had never spoken to him — I hadn't wanted to show off my ignorance. The prof turned back around, saw the mistake, and told me I was right. That's when I knew I really got it.

I also caught a break. The failed mid-term mark was worth only 10 percent of the final grade. I aced the final exam worth the other 90 percent. Ironically, Calculus III was my highest mark at McGill.

So here's what I learned: In 30 years of working with people, I have often seen those whose attitude ensures failure. They assume they will fail, and then they do. It's a self-fulfilling prophecy. Others believe they will succeed, and they do succeed. It's another self-fulfilling prophecy. While I may not have thought I was going to fail Calculus III, in the end it took a change of perspective — literally — for me to succeed.

In a similar vein, how we view the world, to a large extent, can affect our successes or failures in life (or in Calculus III, for that matter). If your perspective isn't getting you what you want, reframe it. Visualize things differently — just like the z axis.

10. People Are Not Simple

I know enough of the world now to have almost lost the capacity of being much surprised by anything.

Charles Dickens

When I used to conduct training sessions for the implementation of new computer systems, invariably one of the attendees would complain about complexity at some point. I would argue that the system designs were intentionally complex, but that complexity or simplicity was in the eye of the beholder. Complexity in the system usually means simplicity for the user.

At Hyundai, the Global Human Resources team would meet annually, usually in Korea. We were a group of about 40 senior HR professionals from around the world and an equal number of HR staff from various levels of the parent company. The last time I attended, the organizers had arranged for us to tour the main Hyundai production facility in Ulsan, at the southern end of the Korean peninsula.

From an engineering perspective, the facility was breathtaking. As we rode through it by bus — walking would have been out of the question due to the sheer size — we drove past thousands of industrial robots performing incredibly complex manoeuvres, repeatedly, unfailingly producing precise welds or bends in sheet metal depending on the task at hand. It was humbling to experience the complexity of what I was seeing. I was travelling with a group of fellow professionals who did nothing more complex than developing compensation systems or organizing holiday functions for our companies.

Then it struck me, like the systems analogy. I watched each arc weld being produced at exactly the same location over and over again as a new sheet of metal passed by the robotic arm, each input and output the same as the previous one. Input in, output out. I knew exactly what was going to happen. I then reflected on the complexity of the machines that the forty of us were dealing with on a day-to-day basis. We could say the same thing to two people and get completely different reactions from each. In fact, we could say the same thing to a person on two days and get a completely different reaction from that person on each day. Input in, output … who knows. Not so simple.

Gerald Knight was the President of one of the engineering firms I worked for, and he loved to work with organizational charts. He would sit and move boxes around forever, trying to find the right mix of who should report where, how many people should work for whom, and the like. Partly, what he was doing was important in succession planning and the day-to-day strategy of running the business. But Gerald's underlying assumption was that if you moved boxes and the people associated with them around, you could solve problems without creating others. I need a skill set over here — move it there — problem solved. It was very linear thinking, but people aren't linear.

Andrew Ellison was a favourite of Gerald. Andrew was seen by most in the company as the person with the greatest potential — someone who could one day assume the top job in the organization. Andrew was an engineer and an MBA. He worked well with a variety of people and was almost universally liked.

He had originally joined the company in a field position that required frequent travel and visits to client sites. His potential was noted, especially by Gerald, and Andrew was originally brought in to Head Office to head up the Business Development function. Through a subsequent series of rapid head-office promotions, Andrew assumed the top job in Marketing, the VP role. It was an amazing rise for someone in his early thirties and very unusual in the company's conservative environment where age, experience, and paying your dues were extremely important.

Harold Morrison was also well respected. Harold had worked for the company previously, left to join a competitor, and rejoined the company to head up the Planning function several years later. He was also an MBA. He had a tendency to be a bit abrasive to those not in his group, but nevertheless, the people who worked for him felt a strong sense of loyalty.

After a few years in the Planning function, Harold was asked to head up the Ontario Marketing Region. Ontario was the largest potential market for the company, but for a variety of reasons, historically it had lagged behind other regions. Harold's challenge was to turn the region around and build it up to assume a market leadership position. Over a five year period he did just that; Harold's work made Ontario the leading region in Canadian sales. But after five years, he was getting restless, and he told Gerald that he wanted to move into something else.

Gerald sat down with his organization charts and started to move boxes around. At this point Harold, as Ontario Manager, reported to Andrew as VP Marketing. Gerald reasoned that if the two positions were swapped, both men would benefit. Harold could take his experience and knowledge running his region to a national level and implement some of the changes that worked in Ontario to the entire country. And Andrew, who had never actually had the responsibility of running a region, could gain the valuable experience that he would need to assume even greater responsibility. Harold's restlessness would be overcome, and a perceived gap in Andrew's resume would be addressed. It looked like a win-win for everyone. But people are not so simple. Input in, output ... who knows.

After about a year of the new reporting structure, Andrew resigned. He left for another opportunity, officially saying that he wanted to gain experience in an area that was new to him. Andrew told me, though, that the real reason he had looked at other options was that he believed he had been demoted. He never bought Gerald's explanation about building up the experience he lacked.

Harold, in addition to his marketing role, was later put in charge of a major systems implementation project that was floundering. He wore two hats and became increasingly stressed, and this pressure ultimately led to his departure. Within an 18-month period, Gerald had lost two talented managers and a big part of the future of the company.

So here's what I learned: As you begin your career, understand that at every step you take, you'll be working with people, and you'll depend on others for your success. But people aren't linear or simple. Never assume that someone will do what you expect them to, even if you know them well. If you need to make a decision that will impact others, get their input first. You may not like their answers, and you may not accept their suggestions in the end, but at least you won't be taken by surprise.

11. Loyalty Is Not Dead

I'll take fifty percent efficiency to get one hundred percent loyalty.

Samuel Goldwyn

I worked for several years with Isabelle Morrison. Isabelle's husband, Brad, grew up in Montreal like I did and was a huge fan of our beloved Montreal Canadiens. I knew instinctively that Isabelle and Brad were raising their children, Olivia and Liam, properly: Liam had become a hockey nut who also lived and died with the fortunes of his favourite team — the Montreal Canadiens. One Christmas he asked his parents for a hockey sweater — and not just any sweater. He wanted the sweater of … Sidney Crosby. Wait, what? Sidney Crosby, of the dreaded Pittsburgh Penguins?

"Yeah, dad," Liam said. "He's my favourite player. I still like the Canadiens, but I want to wear Crosby's jersey."

Now in my day, this would have been considered sacrilege; wearing the colours of another team would have been out of the question. And maybe one day young Liam will see the light and come back to his senses. But I doubt it. Loyalty just doesn't mean what it once did.

After coming to Canada from his native Europe, my dad worked essentially for two organizations. As I was growing up he was the

Buyer for a furniture manufacturer in Montreal, Ideal Upholstering. He worked for the Singer family — the owners of the company — for twenty-five years. And I believe he would have retired with them had the company not gone bankrupt. He would work five and a half days a week, always going in on Saturday mornings, and never once, to my knowledge, did he consider leaving. After the company went under, he worked at another job until he retired. So in his entire working career, my dad was completely loyal to both of his organizations.

My father's experience was not that unusual for his generation. Following World War II, there was an implicit contract between workers and their companies: you would be loyal to the organization you worked for, and unless you really screwed up badly, you would have a job for life.

When I started my career that "contract" still existed to an extent, but the landscape was changing. For a variety of reasons — globalization and other economic forces chief among them — the concept of a lifetime contract was disappearing. Companies began laying off their workers. In some cases it was so they could continue to compete globally, but in other cases it was purely for short-term economic gain. That broke the "contract." If an organization couldn't be counted on for loyalty to its staff, why would the staff commit their loyalty to the organization? Workers began to look for better deals elsewhere.

Today you often hear companies lament that loyalty is dead. The kids entering the workforce today are only in it for themselves. I would suggest, however, that loyalty is not dead. The concept of loyalty has changed.

Andrew Ellison was one of the rising stars in our engineering firm. In a series of promotions, he had progressed to the top marketing job in the organization. Andrew was an engineer in his early thirties and was the de facto leader of a group of younger staff within the company.

Two of the members of Andrew's group were also engineers who had moved over to the marketing side. Two others were managers —

both promising stars in the organization who had advanced to roles of responsibility more quickly than would normally be expected in the conservative engineering environment. All four of them were "Andrew's guys" (though technically, one of them wasn't a guy).

The company decided for a variety of reasons to move Andrew into a role that seemed like a demotion, both to Andrew and to most of the rest of the company. After about a year in the new role, Andrew resigned from the company to pursue other opportunities. He told me that the real reason he was leaving was because he felt he had been "screwed over" by the company. Apparently, so too did "Andrew's guys." Within 18 months, each of them left the firm in succession. The departure of five key staff members — three of whom were managers on the fast track — left a huge void in the succession plan.

Why did they leave? I would suggest it was out of loyalty. It may not be the same brand of loyalty that my dad exhibited to his organizations or that I display by wearing my team's colours, but there's a different concept of loyalty at play — a loyalty to individuals, as opposed to organizations.

I think this shift stems from two sources. First, my kids' generation has been witness to the breaking of the "work for life" contract. They have seen their parents' generation leave or be left by their organizations. I never witnessed that with my dad — nor did most of the rest of my generation. Second, I believe our society currently subscribes to the cult of personality, such that we are attracted to individuals, as opposed to the groups they represent.

The question is whether this shift in loyalty is a good thing, and I would argue it is. The trade union movement began in the early 1900s as a means to rein in the excesses and absolute power of employers, and it helped to create much of the legislation and business ethos that is intended to protect workers. But the movement seems to have run its course, and union membership has been in decline for many years. This new concept of loyalty, I believe, has replaced the trade unions in reining in excesses and absolute power of employers today. Mess with one person in your organization, and you are likely to be messing with a bunch of people — to the detriment of the whole.

So here's what I learned: Just as it is important for kids to have the "right" friends and form the "proper" values at an early age, it is important to consider the "right" groups and associations within the organizations you join. Get into the right groups, and you are more likely to maintain career security. Business is, after all, a people game and the connections you make are vital.

And by the way, if I see you in other than a Canadiens jersey, I'm still going to be pissed.

12. You Don't Owe Your Heart

You've got to give loyalty down, if you want loyalty up.

Donald T. Regan

My favourite movie is *Twelve Angry Men*, in which Henry Fonda plays the main protagonist, Juror #8. Unnamed until the final scene, Fonda's character is the lone holdout against the conviction of a street kid in the murder of his father. Spoiler alert... over the course of the film, Fonda's character eventually persuades all of the others on the all-male jury (the original film was made in 1957) to his side using a variety of classic influence techniques aimed either at the head or the heart, depending on the individual he is trying to convince.

I was introduced to the film during the first week of Western's MBA program, and I subsequently learned that law schools and other programs use the movie to illustrate the persuasion techniques used. In the HR world, or in any profession where the ability to influence others to your point of view is required, these techniques are critical.

The head versus the heart — it's a classic dilemma. Some people tend to make decisions on a purely logical basis (the head) while others are moved to decide based on emotional appeals (the heart).

But the head–heart dichotomy exists in organizations as well, expressed in a variety of ways. Much has been written about the distinction between involvement and commitment within organizations. The difference is illustrated in an old joke about a bacon-and-egg breakfast — the chicken is involved in the breakfast; the pig is committed. The distinction is also true at the individual level in a boss–subordinate relationship. What does the subordinate owe the boss? Is it the head, the heart, or both?

I worked at Hyundai Auto Canada twice during my career – the first time in the early 1990s and subsequently about twenty years later. Hyundai is a global conglomerate based out of Korea with subsidiaries all over the world. It is involved in a number of industries, including automobile manufacturing, steel making, and shipbuilding, among many others.

In local Hyundai affiliates, it was typical for a team of expatriate staff from head office to oversee local operations and liaise back to Seoul for a term of three to five years. They were known as Korean Coordinators, and each team was headed up by a senior staff member from the parent organization. All of the Korean Coordinators had dual reporting relationships — both to the local senior staff member and to the line manager back in Korea.

Korean society, I learned during my two stints at Hyundai, is very paternalistic. There is a distinct pecking order, and what the top guy says goes. There may have been some discussion — very careful discussion — between the parties, but ultimately everyone deferred to the word of his senior (and they are almost always male).

Some would look at this relationship as one of unwavering commitment to the boss. I don't see it that way.

I was originally hired into Hyundai by the company President, who had just completed his fourth year in Canada. In the three weeks between my acceptance of the offer and my agreed start date, the president was reassigned back to Korea and his replacement was sent to Canada.

The President who returned to Korea, I learned later in discussions with others in the company, was revered by the Canadian staff. He was easygoing and soft-spoken — most people considered him a nice guy. And he was totally immersed in the Canadian operation, often working late into the evening.

His replacement was his antithesis. He was aloof, cold, and no nonsense. People steered clear of him as much as they could.

Given these observations, I was surprised to learn from my Korean Coordinator that the Korean staff loved working for the replacement and hated working for the original President, though they deferred fully to both.

For one thing, the new President didn't put in the same long hours at the office — he left relatively early. In the Korean model, it isn't proper to leave the office before your boss, so while the old President was putting in the hours, his subordinates were "stuck."

When the new President left early, so too did the Coordinators. They allowed just enough time for the boss's car to clear the parking lot. To the Canadian operation at the time, the Coordinators were merely involved. In other words, they were "chickens" in terms of their contributions to Hyundai's bacon and eggs.

Twenty years later, the landscape had changed slightly. The president's office was headed by a Canadian, but he had a Korean counterpart who was heavily involved in all aspects of the Canadian operation. All of the Korean expatriates reported through him.

One morning when I arrived at work, I passed by the office of one of the Korean Coordinators. He was in pretty rough shape — slightly dishevelled and with bags under his eyes. It was not that unusual to see the Coordinators in that state, usually when the company was visited by guests from the head office. In the Korean custom, it is very common for the expatriates to invite their guests for a night of drinking and socializing late into the night. I asked the Coordinator who was in town.

"Nobody," he said. "Our boss flew back to Korea last night and all of the Coordinators went out to celebrate." Clearly they were deferential but not necessarily committed.

Lessons Learned

Organizations are full of people who will follow instructions and obey orders from superiors, but these same people would leave at the drop of a hat for a better opportunity. Why? Because superiors can demand obedience, but they can't demand loyalty. Loyalty can only be earned. Organizations are owed only the head, but leaders have the capacity to earn the heart.

So here's what I learned: When you join an organization, you must obey — unless what you're asked to do is immoral, unethical, or illegal (in which case, you must leave).

You *may* be loyal, but that depends on the actions of your boss. If your boss helps you to grow, provides encouragement, allows you to fail and learn from your mistakes, and treats you with respect and dignity, by all means, give him or her your loyalty. If not, don't look back when you leave.

And when you reach a position in your career where people are subordinate to you in a hierarchy, never confuse their obedience with their loyalty. The head and the heart are very different things.

13. The World Isn't Entitled to Your Opinion

Feedback is the breakfast of champions.

Ken Blanchard

I love poker. To be successful at poker, a good player understands that he needs to have a solid grasp of strategy, resource allocation, decision making, persuasion techniques, and psychology. The good player also understands that even if he plays well and makes technically perfect decisions, there is still a possibility that he'll lose. The element of luck, while not the determining factor of success in the long run, will play a significant role in the short run. All of that sounds like the world of business.

I used to play poker in a regular Friday-night game. And anyone who has ever played in a regular poker game knows "The Windbag." The Windbag is the person in the group who, after each hand is played, has an opinion about what everyone should have done. And not only does he have an opinion, he lets the entire group know it — loudly and incessantly.

Anyone who has played with The Windbag wants to shoot him — not just because his opinions are annoying, even if they're technically right, but because the whole point of the game is to win money from the other players around the table. And any advice that you give the "fish," as they are known in the poker world, actually hurts your chances of taking their money. The thing is, The Windbag knows this, but he can't help himself. He thinks that the world is entitled to his opinion. Unfortunately, that too sounds like the world of business.

Over the years, I've conducted many training sessions regarding the use of effective feedback. Feedback — both positive and negative — is essential to the health of any organization. In order for people to develop and grow, they have to both learn from their mistakes and receive recognition for jobs well done. And in order for the organization or subgroup within the organization to meet their objectives, everyone must be aware of whether their actions are on the right track. Feedback is the mechanism for this awareness. But a person who expresses opinions without the intent of truly helping another person grow and develop or keeping an organization on track is nothing more than the corporate version of The Windbag.

I once worked for a boss who was a micromanager. He would not only tell me what he wanted me to do but also how to do it — in great detail. He would tell me how to run my department, who to hire, and who to let go. Among other behaviours, he would point out every miniscule flaw or error in my work, down to a comma used in an internal note. He would move the columns around in the reports that I would provide to him. He would make these changes whether they were relevant to accomplishing the overall task at hand or not, simply because he could. He was the boss, and the world was entitled to his opinion.

Unfortunately, micromanagement in the workplace can have a stifling effect on both the organization and the individuals who work there. In the book *Drive*, by Daniel Pink, the author describes the three key components that motivate people to do their best work — Mastery, Purpose, and Autonomy. We all want to become expert in something that we do; we want to do it for a cause greater than ourselves; and we want to do it by ourselves, without interference, as much as possible. Micromanagement takes Autonomy out of the equation and stifles the Drive — and ultimately the performance — of those who work in that environment. And at the organizational level, micromanagement tends to create a culture of fear and blame, and the growth and development of future leaders are stunted.

I worked for another boss who was the antithesis. He didn't hold back on his feedback, especially when I messed up, but I always had the sense that he was legitimately trying to help me to improve. His comments were specific, relevant, and important to the big picture of what he was trying to build. The people who worked for him became leaders — not only in that company, but throughout the industry.

So here's what I learned: When you are applying for a job, try to ascertain the style of the person you'll be working for. If possible, talk to others who work for that person or have worked for him or her in the past. If you hear that the individual may be a micromanager, think long and hard before accepting the position. Working in that environment can be a nightmare, and ultimately your performance will suffer and your growth will be stunted.

When you get into a position where you supervise others, don't become The Windbag. If you want to express your opinion, make sure that it's either with the intent of helping another person to develop or to keeping something of value to you or to the organization on track. Give feedback that is specific and timely, and allow those who work for you the opportunity to breathe.

The world isn't entitled to your opinion. Most people couldn't care less what you think unless there's something in it for them. One of the surest ways to antagonize others is to give them your opinion without it having been requested.

14. Don't Lie on Your Resume

If you add to the truth, you subtract from it.

The Talmud

Bobby Hearst was a classmate of mine in high school. Bobby was one of the cool group; I was a mix between jock and nerd. We didn't have much in common. I didn't know him all that well, but we were at the smallest school in Montreal. Our graduating class was only about 80 people, so we all managed to keep track of each other to some extent — academic performance, outside interests, and the like. I knew Bobby was interested in journalism.

    Several years later, I worked in a recruiting role at the *Calgary Herald*. It was my first job out of school, and I was just learning the ropes about the Human Resources function. A major part of the job was reviewing resumes — lots of them. To practise, I would start with the resumes of people who had been with the newspaper and were successful, so as to pick up clues about what I might notice on a good resume. The department had kept all of its files for years, long after they should have been archived, and I had access to all of them. I came across one file from the early 1960s on a student, Charles Joseph Clark, who had worked at the *Herald* for a brief period during the summer. "Joe," as he was later known, was Canada's Prime Minister at the time I was reviewing his student resume.

One of my first assignments was to hire a summer intern — the same position that Joe Clark had occupied years before. In those days, most positions were advertised in the local papers, and being the local paper itself, the *Herald* was able to place prominent ads at no cost. We had a tremendous response to the ad we placed for the internship — close to 400 applicants. One of the applicants' names immediately caught my eye: Robert (Bobby) Hearst.

His cover letter was well crafted, as was his resume. It spoke of his many accomplishments, including the fact that he had been the editor of his high school newspaper. Unfortunately for Bobby Hearst, he had the misfortune of finding the one person in Human Resources in the Canadian newspaper industry who knew he was lying. We didn't have a high school newspaper. That little "oops" on his resume cost Bobby his shot with the *Herald*.

Several years later, I worked at the National Cheese Company, starting up their Human Resources function. It was a small, family-run company, and many of the staff had been with them for years. Our Office Manager and Chief Accountant was one of them — and he looked like he had worked there since the first cheese was produced in biblical times. When he finally decided to retire, I began the search for his replacement. We had a fairly good response to our ad and narrowed the selection to three choices — all of whom looked great on paper. And all three interviewed quite well, but Bobby Hearst and his resume had stuck with me.

Because of Bobby, as part of the reference-check process, I called the universities the candidates had attended (or claimed to have attended), as well as the provincial accounting association. Candidate 1 never attended school, and Candidate 2 didn't have the accreditation he had claimed. We hired Candidate 3, Ron Kraft.

I took Ron out for lunch on the day he started. He asked why he had been the successful candidate. I said, "Basically, Ron, these things come down to fit." I didn't want to tell him that he was the only candidate who hadn't lied through his teeth on his resume.

Many years later, I was the Human Resources Manager at Stone & Webster Canada. The company was extremely busy and we had a desperate need for a Construction Manager to head up a series of jobs for us. Most construction people come out of the "School of Hard Knocks" — at the time, even those at the management level. So when our head of construction came to me with a resume from a gentleman with an Honours degree in business, he was very excited. We arranged for the applicant to come in and meet with the construction department and then with me.

The construction department completed the initial interview and brought the candidate up to my office. My first impression was not exactly positive, but you're taught in the recruiting business not to allow first impressions to eliminate what might be a good candidate in the end. His handshake was limp and as soggy as a fish. He never made eye contact, and throughout the interview he was sweating profusely. It was clear he was incredibly nervous, and I could not imagine him in charge of a team of construction workers. My final impression didn't differ much from my initial, and I told the department head so after the interview. But he needed a construction manager.

There was something that was still really bothering me about the candidate though. I just couldn't put my finger on it. I reviewed his resume again. He had an Honours degree from The Trinity University. Wait... not Trinity College at the University of Toronto. I quickly googled "The Trinity University," and I found it. It was a matchbook school based out of Spain that granted degrees for a $2,000 fee (medicine excluded). For $500 extra, you could graduate with honours. I pointed out my findings to the construction department, and our search continued.

So here's what I learned: Don't lie on your resume. Learn how to write a good one, for sure. Spruce it up — make yourself look good. However, understand that your resume serves only as a means to get you in or out of the interview process. At the end of the day, you have to imagine that everything you write will be checked, and you'd better be able to defend what you claim. You may never run into the only person in Canada who knows you're lying. But my working assumption is that you will.

15. Interviews Can Be Challenging

During job interviews, when they ask: "What is your worst quality?" I always say: "Flatulence." That way I get my own office.

Dan Thompson

The strangest interview I ever sat through was my introduction to Hyundai. It was actually the second of three interviews I would have with the company. The first meeting had been with Benjamin Chan. Ben was the Chief Operating Officer at the time, the highest ranking Canadian in the company. The President was an employee of Hyundai Motor Company — the Korean parent. My initial meeting with Ben was routine, and he obviously felt that I had enough to contribute that he asked me to come back a second time.

On the second visit, Ben led me into the company boardroom where he asked me to wait for the President. I waited, and I waited — about fifteen minutes, as I recall. Finally the boardroom door opened and three Korean gentlemen, along with Ben, assumed seats around the table. Ben made brief introductions and then said nothing more for the duration of the interview. In fact, there was only one other individual who spoke at all — the President.

I don't recall the first question, but I do remember it required only a very short answer. I answered — to a wall of silence. No one moved. And we waited. About a minute later – and it seemed much longer — the President asked his second question. Same pattern. I answered very simply, to stony silence and seemingly blank stares. And we waited. I could almost hear crickets chirping. Question three was the same, followed by about ten others. Some of the questions were unique to my experience — what did my father do for a living, and how long had my parents been married. I remember thinking that this was quite strange and, from an HR perspective, pretty illegal — and I was tired. I didn't know if it was an interview "game," but if it was, I decided to play along. I answered each question in turn honestly, directly, and briefly, and then I sat in silence to wait for the next one. If you've ever tried it, it's not easy to sit for long stretches without wanting to fill the void. But I did.

Finally and without notice, the President stood up — after which we all did. He shook my hand and said thank you, and he and the two other Koreans left. I slumped back into my chair and said to Ben: "Wow, that was truly awful." He responded with a smile: "You did great!"

After a brief meeting the next day to discuss terms and conditions, Hyundai made me an offer.

That experience was my first of many introductions to intercultural differences in business — but not to weird interviews. I had previously learned, and continue to learn, that the world is full of people who can't conduct good interviews. Unfortunately they think they can.

During my interview for medical school, I was asked how life is like a field of wheat. Obviously I missed that answer because I'm not a doctor.

My favourite bad interview story (of many) took place when I was at Western. In second year of the business program, employers were scheduled to come on campus to meet with the students during a three-week period. Sign-up sheets were posted, and after a review of student resumes, companies would choose who they wanted to interview.

Many of my classmates were highly sought after and marketable. Some had interviews scheduled each day of the three-week period. One of my classmates — whom I won't name because he's quite successful now and might not appreciate the story — had just finished a session with Imperial Oil on the last day of the on-campus visits. He was one of the marketable ones, and this was his final interview after about fifteen or so. We were in the campus pub comparing interview notes. He laughed and said, "Well, I'm definitely not working for Imperial Oil. I sort of threw the interview."

"What do you mean you threw it?" I asked.

"Look, I've been in interviews for the last three weeks," he said. "I knew what they were going to ask before they asked it. And I had decided pretty early on that I wasn't interested in working for them, so I waited for it — and it came. 'What is your greatest strength?' So I gave them one of my stock answers. And guess what came next. 'What is your greatest weakness?' At this point, I had had it with the same stupid questions, so I said, 'little girls with big boobs.'"

Needless to say, that ended the interview and his career success did not come from working at Imperial Oil.

Unfortunately, that Imperial Oil interview is not uncommon. I have spent nearly 30 years in positions requiring interviewing others. Many of those interviews have been conducted with senior managers who are convinced that they can reach into a candidate's soul and know them after a half hour initial meeting. For years they rely on pet questions, without realizing that these stock inquiries have no relevance to the process of finding the best person for the position.

They have pet questions; I have pet-peeve questions.

My least favourite of the stock questions you are likely to come across is this one: "Where do you see yourself five years from now?" (Substitute another number in variations.)

The problem I have is this: there is no right answer. Either the candidate has no ambition, too much ambition, or just the right amount of ambition but with an over-rehearsed answer. On top of that, I have known the same senior managers to reject different candidates for any one of those three sins.

So here's what I learned: Over the course of your career, you're going to be interviewed by many people. Many of these interviews will be conducted by people who aren't skilled interviewers. There are many excellent books that provide stock answers to typical interview questions. Read them, but understand what is required to succeed in the position being offered, and develop your own themes and specific answers around your own stories. You're going to have to help out many of your interviewers because their questions won't always help them to see all that you can offer them.

Oh, and bend, but don't break. Just like wheat in a wheat field — which mirrors life you know.

16. Learn to Tell a Compelling Story

After nourishment, shelter, and companionship, stories are the thing we need most in the world.

Philip Pullman

When I was working at TGO Consulting, I was a Senior Consultant and part of the larger Professional Services Team. The team was comprised of the consultants, the developers, and the project managers.

Once a month, we would all meet in the conference room to learn about the progress of projects on the go, what projects were in the pipeline, what new product offerings were coming down the pike, and the like. I found these sessions very helpful. The PS Team were usually out at client sites, and our opportunities to interact with one another were fairly limited. These meetings allowed us, at a minimum, to see each other. But I thought the meetings could be better.

I suggested to the group that collectively we had an incredible amount of experience sitting around the table. We came from a variety of backgrounds and had a wide range of knowledge beyond what we each did at TGO. And we had a variety of personalities —

some of the team members were too shy to speak up in a group setting, even though they capably provided knowledge and expertise to their clients one-on-one. I thought we might be able to take better advantage of that experience, knowledge, and skill by going around the table and "forcing" everyone to provide a "lesson learned" story. The suggestion was accepted, and from that point on, the PS meeting ended with a round-table sharing of lessons learned.

It worked and it didn't work. Everyone did get the chance to speak and to share. But many people, unused to storytelling, would talk about a new technology or the fact that the release of a piece of software was delayed. Oftentimes, someone would get on a roll and take up all of our allotted time talking about how to perform a certain task.

All of these things may have been important on some level, but I wanted to hear their stories. I wanted to really learn from them.

On September 11, 2006, the scheduled day of the Professional Services Team meeting, the meeting progressed in the normal manner with project updates, new technologies, and the like. We progressed around the table in a counter-clockwise direction for our "lessons learned" session, and most of the team talked about technology or the issues they were having with a particular client. I was second-last to speak.

When it was my turn, I started by saying that my story was a bit old but, I thought, still relevant.

"Five years ago today, I was in a taxi driving to the airport," I began. "I was scheduled to take a transcontinental flight to a meeting in Calgary. Over the radio, I listened as the second World Trade Center Tower collapsed. At that point I knew that I wasn't going to fly anywhere that day. And I was in no mood to go back to the office I had left 10 minutes earlier. I asked the cab driver to take me home. I wanted to be home when my wife got there, and I wanted to be able to pick up my kids from school. On that day, the only thing that mattered to me was that we were a family, we were together, and we were safe. So my 'lesson learned' is this — and I think it's as relevant today as it was five years ago. No matter what frustrations you have with a client, what issues you have with software or hardware, what business may or may not be coming in, at the end of the day the only things that truly matter are your family, that you're together, and that you're safe."

When I finished, there was silence in the room, and when I looked around, most of the group were wiping away tears. The last to speak was one of our project managers. She said simply: "After that, I got nothing."

As I write this, I am many years removed from telling that story. But I guarantee that the majority of the people in that room that day can tell you where I was on September 11, 2001. They can tell you that long after they can tell you any of the facts, figures, updates, or issues that were raised at that meeting.

So here's what I learned: Learn to tell a story. It's how we, as humans, relate to each other and how we best learn from each other. The ability to tell a compelling story will set you apart from the rest.

17. Get Comfortable in Front of a Crowd

The human brain starts working the moment you are born and never stops until you stand up to speak in public.

George Jessel

Jerry Seinfeld tells this joke: Apparently the two biggest fears people have are 1) public speaking, and 2) death. That means that the guy delivering the eulogy at a funeral wants to trade places with the guy in the casket.

I'm a pretty shy guy. In Myers-Briggs language, I am an introvert — and a pretty strong introvert. As such, speaking in front of a crowd can be uncomfortable. I don't necessarily want to trade places at a funeral, but it's painful nonetheless.

When I studied biochemistry, there were very few opportunities for me to make presentations to groups. Most of the exams were multiple choice and paper-based — no essays, few presentations — just as I liked it. However, I remember one presentation that stuck out. I had to discuss the usage of iodinated uridine, a radioactive compound used in cancer research. Iodinated uridine is represented as "IDU," and I had to concentrate hard to keep from mixing IDU with IUD, the acronym for intrauterine device — something

Lessons Learned

decidedly not used in cancer research. I remember making a mess of it throughout the talk. Those mix-ups didn't help my confidence.

When I attended business school, there was much more emphasis on speaking in groups, and that tended to bring my marks down a little. My class participation grades weren't spectacular.

After graduation, my first few jobs provided fewer opportunities still — until I became the Human Resources Manager at Stone & Webster. Stone & Webster was an organization of 400 people when I joined, and the staff grew to 600 at its peak. There were plenty of opportunities for me to make a fool of myself in front of a crowd.

I remember the first time I addressed an assembly of our staff. We were in the process of changing our pension plan design, and the changes were to be introduced over about two years. For the kick-off meeting to outline the new plan, we didn't have a large enough meeting room to house everyone. Our facilities manager arranged for us to use an empty floor in the office tower where we were located. All eyes were on me as I strode to the podium to begin speaking amid the concrete pillars and hanging wires. When I opened my mouth, very little came out. I started to get pretty light headed and realized I had stopped breathing. Just before I might have passed out, I was able to take a couple of gulps of air to continue. I did pull it off, but the people in the front row surely would have noticed the sweat dripping off my face by the time I had finished.

Shortly after that episode, I attended a Human Resources conference where one of the keynote speakers was a psychologist from the University of Ottawa, Dr. Brian Little. Dr. Little's talk — and I remember it to this day — was entitled "Introverts and Extroverts – Driving Each Other to Distraction." He talked about what introverts do that drives extroverts crazy and vice versa.

He was an incredibly compelling and engaging speaker, and the audience ate him up. He had everyone in the room laughing and whooping and hollering at various points. And then came the kicker: He said, "Guess where I stand on the introvert–extrovert scale."

It was almost unanimous; the room voted him to be an extreme extrovert. "Wrong," he said. "In fact, I am an extreme introvert and a 'closet' extrovert. I have learned to mask my introversion, and I'm actually at the point where I enjoy speaking to groups. But it takes a lot out of me, and I spend a lot of time before and after an event by myself preparing and then recharging." His talk was a revelation to me.

A little while later, I got to try again. Stone & Webster had a tradition of sponsoring a tea for staff who had contributed 25 years of service. Each honouree could invite as many as 25 people, and the tea was served with biscuits in the company boardroom. The President would say a few words about the honouree, recognizing his or her contributions to the company, and we would all clap politely and go our separate ways. It was as dreadfully boring as it sounds, and because there were so many long-term staff at the company, these celebrations happened frequently.

Two of our Chief Engineers hit 25 years within the same week, and their fete was scheduled. On the day of the event, the President fell sick, and because it was a double group of 50 who had committed to be there, he didn't want to cancel. I was asked to host.

The two honourees were really popular and funny guys, and I wanted to try something different from the normal platitudes. I pulled their employee files, which included their entire histories with the company, and crafted a speech comparing what was going on 25 years earlier to what was happening at the present time — photographs included.

O. J. Simpson was on trial for murder at the time, and 25 years earlier he had won the NFL rushing title. Apollo 13 had won the Academy award for the story of an event that had occurred 25 years earlier. There were other freaky coincidences, but the punchline was that the crappy orange carpet and creaky office furniture that everyone in the company hated were the same orange carpet and office furniture from 25 years earlier. As I finished speaking, the place was laughing and whooping — just like in Dr. Little's talk. I realized I could "fake it" just as he could.

Lessons Learned

As part of the conversion of our pension, we had developed a software-based communication tool tailored to help each employee decide whether to stay in the existing plan or move to the new plan. Today, such software is commonplace, but at the time it was only large consulting houses that could provide the same tool. The fact that we had developed this tool and implemented it ourselves made our story fairly compelling to the pension community. For about two years thereafter, I was sought out to speak at pension conferences and discuss our approach. I actually learned to enjoy those speaking engagements — even though before and after each event they were painful for me.

So here's what I learned: There will be times throughout your career when you will have to stand and deliver. Regardless of your personality preferences, get comfortable speaking in public. It's a skill necessary for advancement within organizations. If you prepare properly, you just might find those opportunities to be tremendously rewarding and enjoyable — if a little scary. At least you'll prefer to deliver the eulogy.

18. Make a List

Success requires making a hundred small steps go right — one after the other, no slipups, no goofs, everyone pitching in.

Atul Gawande

I once had the opportunity to fly to Lloydminster, Alberta. "Opportunity" is a bit generous since unless you're from Lloydminster or you work there, there isn't really much of a reason to go. But when I worked with Delta Projects in Calgary, we had been contracted to perform a portion of the remediation of a gas-processing plant there, and I had to visit our staff to discuss changes to our benefit coverage. Lloydminster sits on the Alberta–Saskatchewan border, and there were no regularly scheduled commercial flights from anywhere. To get there quickly, we had to charter a plane.

I flew with several other Delta staff who were scheduled to attend other meetings. We left very early on a Monday morning from Springbank airport, about half an hour outside of Calgary. It was quite dark as we crossed the tarmac to board the plane, and at first it was difficult to see exactly what we would be getting into. Now, I'm no aviation expert — I can't tell you what we flew in. But I do recall the sense that someone had attached wings to a school bus, and this was to be our mode of transportation.

The pilot greeted us as we boarded the plane and informed us that due to flight regulations, one of us would have to "ride shotgun" next to him. I guess I was the slowest to take a step backwards because he pointed to me and said, "You're the volunteer."

As I assumed my seat, I said to him, "Just to be clear, if something happens to you, you do realize that we're all going to die."

He told me not to worry, that he had many years of experience flying these planes into places far more remote than Lloydminster, and that nothing bad was going to happen. This only reassured me so much, especially when he pulled a laminated card out of his flight bag and began to run through a set of pre-flight procedures. I asked him why, if he was so experienced, he would need a checklist to tell him what to do. He told me that, by regulation, every pilot on every flight — regardless of size of aircraft and regardless of air miles flown — has to use his procedures checklist. The flight was uneventful, and I enjoyed my one-week stay in Lloydminster (it was actually only a day, but as the old joke goes it seemed like a week). On the return flight, I was quicker stepping backwards, and one of my colleagues got the jump seat.

Several years later, I was flying a regularly scheduled commercial flight from Toronto to Montreal. I recognized one of the flight attendants to be the wife of one of my best buddies, Sol Hegyi. Sol and I had shared many wacky experiences over the years, including two student tours of Europe. He was the best man at my wedding, and I was in his wedding party when he married Karen the following year. Karen had been flying for many years, but this was the first time I had been on one of her flights.

About fifteen minutes into the trip, Karen approached me and asked whether I wanted to sit in the cockpit — this was obviously pre-9/11. I said that I would love to. Five minutes later, I was sitting in the third seat, behind the pilot and the co-pilot. We chatted about the weather, the news, the previous night's hockey game — anything but the flight. The plane was flying on autopilot, but I still couldn't believe how informal they were until about 15 minutes before we landed. Out came the checklist. Then these guys were all business, and everything revolved around that list. The scene brought me back to that flight to Lloydminster and my interaction with the bush pilot. He was right, it seems — every pilot, no matter the aircraft or the experience, has these lists.

When I worked at Petro-Canada, the company was just getting into the aviation fuel business. I attended a meeting of about twenty people to discuss the policies and procedures around ensuring the quality of the product. One of the marketing guys talked about the kinds of complaints that the company might receive about fuel quality. To which another manager — more experienced with aviation fuels — responded, "You obviously don't understand the situation. The plane lands — no complaints. The plane doesn't land — no complaints."

A number of years later still, I was arranging for the Chairman of Hyundai's jet to land at a private hangar at Toronto's Pearson airport. I worked with the head of operations of the private aviation firm that ran the terminal. In every reference to the flight, he would refer to the passengers as "souls."

"We have a plane scheduled to arrive at Pearson with seven souls on board," he radioed to his assistant. Souls — not guests, not people, not passengers, but souls.

The aviation industry — the industry that insists that every pilot no matter how experienced must use a checklist to ensure they get it right — refers to their passengers as souls.

So here's what I learned: In your career you will be in many situations where you must "get it right." These may or may not be life and death situations, but they may, nevertheless, be critical to your career success. No matter how experienced you become, if it's essential you get it right, follow the aviation industry's lead and use a checklist.

19. The Complications of Culture and Language

By suppressing differences and peculiarities, by eliminating different civilizations and cultures, progress weakens life and favours death.

Octavio Paz

I worked with Hyundai Auto Canada on two occasions separated by about twenty years. The first time I joined them in the mid-1980s, I knew I would get to experience work life very differently than I had until then. At the time, there wasn't much written about Korean culture and doing business in Korea and with Koreans. That has changed now, but back then I picked up a book about Japanese business culture. There was much being written at the time about Total Quality Management, *Kaizen*, and how North American businesspeople could learn from the Japanese model. I assumed that Japanese and Korean cultures would be the same. I was right and I was wrong.

My first boss at Hyundai was the President. His appointment to the top of the Canadian organization seemed unusual from my perspective; he had risen through Hyundai Motor Company, our parent in Korea, primarily through the Human Resources division — not the typical path to the top of a North American company.

Initially I enjoyed working for him. He was quite open with his time and he must have considered me somewhat of a protegé as I was his Human Resources Manager. We would have many lengthy discussions about the differences and similarities between Korean and Canadian cultures, attitudes toward work and family, and life in general. During one of these meetings he said to me, "You think too North American. I am going to send you to Korea." True to his word, a month later he put me on a plane to Seoul.

I spent about a week in Korea and had a chaperone assigned to me — a young mid-level manager from Hyundai Motor Company who was similar in age to me. We had some fascinating discussions about each other's cultures, and some of my misconceptions about Japanese and Korean environments were dispelled. I guess I didn't learn enough because when I returned, the President still felt I thought "too North American." I became tired of the structured and hierarchical ways that he ran the company, and our relationship deteriorated. I left about nine months after my return from Korea.

I rejoined the company about twenty years later when I thought the landscape might have changed.

One thing that hadn't changed in the interim was the system of Korean Coordinators. The Coordinators were typically mid to senior level managers from Hyundai Motor Company, assigned overseas on assignments lasting up to five years. The company's stated purpose for these positions was to act as a liaison between the head office and overseas subsidiaries. In reality, they had much more of a decision-making role. For each Canadian Manager, there was a Korean Coordinator, and decisions were typically made jointly. Much of the career success at Hyundai from a Canadian Manager's perspective depended on forming a good working relationship with the Coordinator. Otherwise life would be very frustrating — or worse.

I had several Coordinators during my two stints at Hyundai. One of them was Harvey Kim, a finance guy in the parent company. When he was assigned to Canada, he took over the role of Chief

Financial Officer for the Canadian subsidiary without assuming the actual title. But he also became Coordinator for the Legal and Human Resources groups.

I ended up getting to know Harvey fairly well in the three or so years we spent together, and I quite liked him. We shared a mutual interest in sports, especially tennis — that was his game. He would talk of the battles between Federer and Nadal the same way I would talk about the previous night's hockey game. His English was pretty good — he understood almost everything. Sometimes, though, communication issues did arise.

Soon after his arrival, I sensed that a number of the staff, in both the Human Resources and Finance departments, were very uncomfortable dealing with Harvey. I made a purposeful effort to see if I could determine why. One day I listened in to a number of conversations he was having, and after a few of these discussions the problem became clear. I called Harvey into my office and closed the door.

In the movie *The Princess Bride*, one character constantly uses the word "inconceivable" incorrectly. There's a scene where another character says to him, "I don't think that word means what you think it means." Our discussion went like that.

I said, "Harvey, when you talk to people, you're threatening them. You say they 'better' do this or 'better' do that. I don't think that word means what you think it means. In English there is a hierarchy—" I illustrated by moving my hand upward. "—could do, should do, must do, better do. Better do is a threat."

Harvey blanched. "No, no," he said. Now it was his turn to illustrate, moving his hands. "…better do, could do, should do, must do. I'm saying I think it's better if they do this."

Once he got it, it was an easy fix and the relationships between all of us improved.

So here's what I learned: Over the course of your career you will, to an even larger extent than I did, work with people from various cultures, who speak various languages, and who come from all over the world. Sometimes you may think you know what someone is saying, and you will infer a meaning very different from that which was intended because of the vagaries of our language. Don't climb the "ladder of inference." Instead, go back and check your assumptions. There are actually far greater differences between individuals of the same culture than between individuals of different cultures. We're all human at the end of the day.

20. Just Say Thanks

I would maintain that thanks are the highest form of thought, and that gratitude is happiness doubled by wonder.

G. K. Chesterton

Bob Branch and I worked together for many years. Bob was an engineer, but he didn't exactly fit the image that tends to conjure up. It's true that he once explained the concept of "harmonic motion" to me in the middle of a fire drill, using our escape in the stairwell of our office building as an example. Later, back in my office, he related the theory to an IndyCar race in ways that I would never have considered. But in other ways, he seemed quite "normal."

He was very actively involved in local politics and was an elder in his church. It was the latter that brought us together for many memorable discussions.

As observant as Bob was, you might think it unusual that he would have deep philosophical debates with a heathen like me. But he did, and we talked for many hours. I respected his beliefs as much as he seemed to accept my view of the world.

One day, just before the winter break at our office, Bob popped his head in the door and said, "Merry Christmas." When I didn't respond immediately, he asked, "Does my wishing you a Merry Christmas bother you?"

"Actually," I said, "it does." So he stepped into my office and I began to explain why. But before I could get too far into my explanation, another of our staff stopped by and also wished me the best of the season in exactly the same way that Bob had, just minutes earlier.

"Thank you, John, and Merry Christmas to you and your family as well," I replied, and John toddled off down the hall to continue bidding his holiday message to others.

"Aren't you being a little hypocritical?" Bob said to me.

"Not at all," I replied. "You know exactly what my beliefs are, and yet you said something that you knew might offend me. I know that it's Christmas — I see it and hear it in every store I enter, every second song on the radio, and there's a large decorated tree with fake gifts standing in our foyer. I don't have to be reminded by someone who knows that I don't celebrate it. But John doesn't know me that well. His wishing me a Merry Christmas was like a gift. And I take that exactly in the spirit as he intended it."

Bob thought for a bit and said, "Okay. Happy holidays. Let's talk about this further when we come back in January." And we did.

Several years later, Stone & Webster had just completed a major construction project on time and slightly under budget. It was a huge accomplishment for the company. The job was difficult from a variety of angles — the technology was relatively new, and the client was quite challenging. All this was accomplished at a time that our parent company in Boston was in a financial crisis. So our senior management decided to reward our staff with a gift. It was merely a token, but a gesture that would indicate a job well done by the team. Team ... baseball season ... baseball caps for everyone.

I met with our supplier of logo ware. The company logo was gold, and together the supplier and I looked at a number of different styles and colours of caps. I left the final decision about colour coordination to them, as they were more expert than I (as my family will attest), and they decided to go with a green cap with the gold logo prominently centred.

At the conclusion of the company's next all-employee meeting, as each staff member filed out of the room, the President thanked them for being part of the team, congratulated them on a job well done, and provided each person with a new cap. The mood seemed generally upbeat and it looked like the gift was well received.

After everyone had left the room, the President and I remained behind chatting. One of our Project Managers, Jimmy Chan, approached us with a big grin on his face. "You do know what a green hat signifies in Chinese culture don't you?" he asked.

We didn't.

"In China," said Jimmy, "when a man wears a green hat, it means that his wife or his girlfriend is cheating on him. I don't think I'll be wearing it — but thanks for the gesture. I think it was appreciated by everyone else."

Who knew? Not us, for sure, and we had a bit of a chuckle, until another manager appeared, but he didn't share Jimmy's grin; he was really angry.

"I'm Sikh. I wear a turban. How dare you present me with this — it's an insult," he said and stormed off. Not exactly the reaction we had anticipated when we first thought up the idea for a gift.

So here's what I learned: In today's world you're going to work with many people of different backgrounds and beliefs. It will be impossible to anticipate every offence based on culture that you might inadvertently commit. That's not to say that you shouldn't try to learn as much as you can about other people. And certainly if something is likely to offend another person based on their background, don't do it or say it. But don't beat yourself up for each cultural faux pas you make — because you will make them. Do what you think is best, and learn from your transgressions the next time.

On the other side, if you receive something, tangible or otherwise, that may offend you or that you might not appreciate, take it in the spirit that it was presented. There is only one appropriate response for that hideous sweater, tie, or scarf that you receive on Christmas, Chanukah, Kwanzaa, your birthday, or whenever: "Thank you."

21. Reward Systems Sometimes Don't Reward

"Do this and you'll get that" makes people focus on the "that" not the "this." Do rewards motivate people? Absolutely. They motivate people to get rewards.

Alfie Kohn

When I was going through the interview process for my job as Human Resources Manager at Stone & Webster, I met with their President and CEO. I had met him previously during the initial interview held by Stone & Webster's hiring committee, but this was to be a more comprehensive session so that we could gauge our mutual ability to work together. To get the job, I would have to get past him.

The interview had been going well, I thought. It was a fairly structured format in which he asked a series of questions about my experiences and how I thought I could help their organization. Then he turned the floor over to me to ask him questions. I had come prepared, and I asked a few about his management style and the like, and then I asked what the company's philosophy was regarding pay.

"That's easy," he said. "Here at Stone & Webster we pay for performance."

Maybe it was because I thought the interview was going so well, but I dropped my guard. Before I could check myself, I said, "You know, I bet you don't."

As soon as the words left my mouth, I thought, *brilliant, you just called the President of the company you want to work for a liar.* He scowled at me and said, "What do you mean we don't pay for performance?"

In an attempt to backtrack slightly, I said, "Well, everybody says they pay for performance, but I have known very few organizations that actually do. Maybe Stone & Webster is one of the rare exceptions."

He hired me anyway, which says something either about my ability to recover or his sense of humour. But on the first day of employment when I was shuttled around on the obligatory meet-and-greet with all of the "need-to-know" people, the President remembered. "You told me we don't pay for performance," he said. "I want you to prove it to me."

After I had settled in and figured out where I could find some data, I developed an analysis.

Stone & Webster was until then a very stable organization with many long-term staff. In the late 1970s and early 1980s, the company had been extremely successful in the design and building of nuclear power stations. As a result, they had hired a large group of engineers to perform the required work. The largest cohort of these engineers was hired 10 years before I joined the company, and I decided to take a look at this group. About 25 of them were still with the firm. I knew what their starting salaries had been, and I knew what their salaries were after a decade's worth of pay increases.

The Chief Engineers had also been a very stable group, and all of them had been in their roles or in their departments for over 10 years. I asked each of them to rank the performance of the engineers in my case study who were from their departments. Armed with these five separate lists (Civil, Mechanical, Electrical, Control Systems, and Process Engineering), I met with the Manager of Engineering, who also had been in his role for more than 10 years. I asked him to take the lists and combine them into one, creating a rank ordering of the performance of all 25 of the engineers.

I then conducted a series of correlation analyses, using as many factors as I could think of. I compared performance, age, gender, department, and many others against the salary increases from the cohort's hiring dates to the present day. When I looked at these analyses my suspicions were validated. There was zero correlation between where each of the engineers stood in their performance ranking and the pay increases they had received over the 10 year time frame. Zero. In fact, only one factor showed any significant correlation to pay increase, and it was a very strong correlation. Starting salary. The lower the starting salary, the higher the increases had been over the years and vice versa.

When I look back, the findings were actually obvious if not entirely scientific. First, my numbers were really too small to be a significant sample size, but more importantly my sample was not exactly random. The people I had chosen had been hired 10 years previously, and over the intervening time frame, the company had not thought them to be sufficiently poor performers to get rid of them. On the other hand, the company had not done enough to anger them to the point that they would have left.

At the time, engineers in Ontario received an annual salary survey conducted by the provincial engineering association, so all of the engineers in the company knew where they stood in relation to the market. If the engineers stayed for 10 years, the company had to have compensated them properly compared to the market, or they would have left.

Despite the lack of scientific rigour in my analysis, the President was satisfied that I had proven my point. The company hadn't paid for performance over the years; they had paid what the market dictated.

Over the years I have used a training exercise in many of the team building sessions I have conducted. It's based on the classic philosophical "prisoner's dilemma." Essentially, the activity clearly shows the benefit of cooperation between groups to the success of the entire entity. One of the discussion points that always comes out of the exercise is the effect of the "reward" that I put on the table for the winning team. Participants claim that the instructions are ambiguous, as it is unclear up front whether the winners are at the individual or the group level.

My argument has always been that in every organization I had seen, they said they "paid for performance," by which they meant that they paid for individual performance. Most organizations say the right things about having to work together with no barriers across their company in order to serve their customers effectively. Yet every organization I have worked for put reward systems in place that conflicted, at least to an extent, with the goal of organizational cooperation. At the end of the day, regardless of the reward system they put in place, the company had to "pay the market" in order to retain their people.

So here's what I learned: When you interview for a job, ask the interviewer how their organization determines pay increases. If they say that they pay for performance or something similar, don't call them a liar — you might not be as lucky as I was with Stone & Webster.

But if they combine the "pay for performance" line with "we have no barriers and exist to serve the customer to the best of our ability," ask yourself if they really mean it. If serving others is one of your key values, organizations that erect barriers in the form of competitive incentive systems might not be for you.

22. Understand Data

The temptation to form premature theories upon insufficient data is the bane of our profession.

Sherlock Holmes

Immediately after leaving Stone & Webster, I worked for TGO Consulting, implementing HR and payroll systems. I was assisting a large not-for-profit client, and as part of the systems implementation, I was providing training on the function and design of all their HR modules. When the topic of pay and performance came up, I asked them what their pay philosophy was. The HR Manager said, "Here, we pay for performance."

"Of course you do," I said, and proceeded to tell them the story of the analysis I had done for Stone & Webster regarding their claim to be using a performance driven pay system.

They listened very politely, but as I finished, the Manager said, "That was a beautiful story. But here, we actually do pay for performance."

"Well," I said, "we're in the process of implementing a system that will allow you to access all kinds of data. Let's take a look at what we see when we're done."

We all agreed that when the system was up and running, the first analysis we would do would look at their most recent performance review data in relation to the pay increases awarded at year-end. At the completion of the project, we did the analysis together.

Using pivot tables in Microsoft Excel, we plotted the pay increases by performance scores from the previous year. To my shock, there was a beautiful, almost linear correlation between the increases and the performance scores. The HR Manager exclaimed, "You see, I told you we pay for performance here!"

I was amazed. It seemed I had found the Holy Grail — an organization that actually paid for performance. But being the ornery sort, I began playing with the data a little further. Rather than plotting the size of the salary increases in relation to the levels of performance, I flipped the graph and plotted the performance scores by the employees' levels in the organization. (Obviously the higher the level in the organization, the higher the salary — so the organization level was a proxy for salary.) And what do you think I found...? A beautiful, almost linear correlation. People at the top of the organization received high performance scores; people at the bottom, lower scores.

For a variety of reasons, this made no sense to me. There is an old business axiom known as the "Peter Principle" that states that people tend to rise within organizations to their own level of incompetence. The principle is a bit tongue-in-cheek, but based on this notion, I would have expected, in a fair system, to see an equal distribution of high and low scores regardless of organization level. If anything, I might have expected poorer scores for people at the top. After all, people at the top of an organizational hierarchy, Peter Principle or not, presumably have more difficult jobs with higher learning curves. What I was seeing here was just the opposite. Something else was going on. Clearly the people at the top end were being held to a much looser standard of performance than the people at the bottom end.

I pointed these findings out to the HR Manager and she immediately began looking deeper into their performance review process. Technically, in the end, I had found an organization that paid for performance, but they paid for performance scores rather than for performance itself.

Businesses today are awash in data. As systems become more comprehensive and complex, the availability and variety of data in organizations is staggering. Yet many organizations, large and small alike, are very poor at translating data into information so that meaningful business decisions can be made.

Years later I was waiting to attend a year-end budget meeting with the President and the rest of the senior staff. In the boardroom where the meeting was to be held, a whiteboard displayed the company's objectives for the coming year. At the time, only the head of IT, the President, and I were in the room. "Do either of you know the size of the market we compete in?" the President asked. "You are leaders in this company and it's something you should know." I had no clue, and neither did my IT counterpart.

I was pretty embarrassed, but the answer was on the whiteboard. Our first two objectives included both share of market and units sold. So I did some quick mental gymnastics by dividing one into the other and said: "I'm not sure, but I would guess about 12 million units."

He saw that I had looked at the board and gave me a look that said *nice recovery, pal*. But from that point on, I decided that I would keep close tabs on industry sales data — our own and that of the competition. I wanted to have a better understanding of our business and our competitive position. Industry sales data were available publically, and I began to chart them on a monthly basis. Lots of data.

We also had lots of data from our HR system regarding how much time people spent away from work, and when. Can completely different sets of data be combined into useful information? Not always, but in this case we were actually able to derive meaning that could affect the business.

The market was remarkably cyclical; the peak sales months were April and May, followed by a gradual drop off through the remainder of the year to a low point in December and January.

The company's vacation pattern was also remarkably cyclical. The staff, like most Canadians took the majority of time off in the summer months of July and August. But there was a mini peak in the month of May. Why? The company had a vacation year that ran from June of one year to May of the next, basically because "it had always been that way." The company also had a policy that said that no more than one week's vacation entitlement could be carried over from one vacation year to the next. All surplus entitlement would be forfeit, so naturally people took time off in May rather than lose their entitlements.

May was also the peak buying month of the year — when our customers were in most need of our services. This was not exactly the right time to have a mini peak of absenteeism. It just didn't make sense. But what had previously been nothing but a lot of data had now been converted to information that we could use.

So here's what I learned: Many people have beliefs that just aren't backed up by any empirical evidence. I believe that the future will belong to those who can make sense of the data we're all awash in — whatever industry or field of work — in order to prove or dispel these common beliefs and to add meaningful insight to the argument.

Unfortunately, many people are spooked by data and numbers. Don't be one of those people.

Learn to analyze data. Convert data into information so you can make meaningful decisions that aren't based on pure assumption and speculation. You'll stand out from the crowd.

23. The Importance of Mentorship

If you want to lift yourself up, lift up someone else.

Booker T. Washington

I had been working at Stone & Webster as the head of HR in Canada for about 15 years when the Shaw Group out of Louisiana purchased the company, and control of HR decision-making was increasingly being transferred down south. Between that and the fact that I had been working in the Human Resources field for over twenty years at that point, I felt I needed a change to recharge.

One of my passions had always been systems — not from a technical point of view. I enjoyed looking at workflows and trying to make them better. I have found that, if left alone too long, the ways that an organization does things tend to become ingrained. At some point, these tactics often stop making sense. Technology changes, people change, and priorities change, but too often methods remain the same.

I had asked some of my contacts if they knew of any organizations that might be in need of my skill set, and one of them put me in touch with the principals at TGO Consulting. TGO was a firm specializing in the implementation of business systems for their clients. At the time, they were looking to bolster their Human Resources and Payroll practice, so the timing seemed right. They weren't looking for a "tekkie," per se, but rather someone with HR experience who could correlate client needs to the systems offerings that TGO had.

I loved my experience in the consulting world. I would go into client organizations and see that they were every bit as messed up as the organizations I had worked for — in some cases even more so — and I would suggest and implement solutions to their issues. I didn't always succeed, and there were times when I was scared witless because I wasn't sure what I was doing. But it was the change I had needed. Still, though, something was missing that I couldn't put my finger on. My answer eventually came in an unusual setting.

One Friday afternoon I was at my desk when Elaine called. "Remember, we have a wedding to go to tonight," she said.

I had forgotten, and I really didn't want to go. The week had been particularly tiring, and it was Jackie's birthday. I just wanted to go home, relax, and celebrate with the family. I told Elaine I would rather not go, and as usual, she set me straight. "You're an idiot. You said we'd go ... we have to go." So we went.

It was the wedding of Emily and Jack, and Emily was the daughter of a business colleague of mine. She had worked for us at Stone & Webster for a couple of summers as she attended university. We had chatted a few times and she said she was interested in getting into either HR or marketing when she graduated. As it turned out, several months before her graduation, an entry-level position opened up in our department.

Based on our interactions, I knew I liked Emily. I liked her dad as well, so I arranged for her to come in to interview (yes, sometimes doing favours for someone you like is part of the game). Emily impressed us. She was confident, smart, and funny, and she had a good grasp of the skill sets we were looking for in this position. She won the competition for the job.

Soon after joining Stone & Webster, Emily said that her boyfriend was out of work, and he would take anything. Well, we had "anything." It was an entry-level position in our mailroom, and we brought Jack on board as well. It became pretty obvious from talking with him that he was smart, and over time I could see that Jack's talents were wasted in the mailroom. He had expressed an interest in the pharmaceutical business, and I had some pretty good contacts through Elaine's work. I called them, arranged for them to interview Jack, and he left to start his career in the pharma sector.

Meanwhile, Emily excelled at everything we asked her to do in Human Resources, but after about two years of working with us, she told us her real passion was marketing. She asked if we could we find her something else within the company. We did, and she moved over to the Marketing group.

She excelled there as well, and after about a year, she was headhunted out and into the retail industry. I followed her progress, learning of her rise through various roles and titles when we met for the occasional lunch. We lost contact for a bit, but she tracked me down at TGO and invited me to her wedding. And apparently I had said we would go.

Elaine and I arrived at the wedding venue and were greeted by Emily's dad, Ian. Emily had family attending from all over the world, and Ian introduced us to them one after another. As I was introduced to each person, it seemed I would hear, "Oh, *you're* Paul Farkas." By the fourth or fifth time it happened, I started to think I must owe these people money.

The wedding progressed and soon it came time for the speeches. When it was Ian's turn to speak, he thanked everyone for coming to his daughter's wedding and pointed out specific people in the room — mostly the family members to whom I had been introduced. He thanked them for coming from England, Australia, and wherever. Then he pointed to me. "And for those of you who don't know him," he said, "that's Paul Farkas. Emily considers him her mentor, and she says she wouldn't be where she is in her career without him."

I was floored — the second most shocked person in the room, behind Elaine. I had no idea.

And then it hit me — that's what was missing for me in the consulting world. I would move from one organization to the next forming contacts and relationships, for sure, but never having the opportunity to form the lasting bonds that can only be developed by working in one place for a period of time.

So here's what I learned: Every successful person I know has had a mentor at some point — someone who showed them the ropes and whose example they could follow. Early in your career, seek out an individual whom you admire, and learn as much as you can from them.

On the other hand, as you progress through your career, remember that you will affect others in ways that you might not realize. Always act in a manner that's true to your values, and behave like someone might want to follow you. Whether you realize it or not, others are watching.

24. Play to Your Strengths

If you have a talent, use it in every way possible.

Brendan Francis

When I was in the MBA program at Western, the students formed study groups. These groups were intended to lessen the burden on each individual — the daily case load review was onerous, and the ability to work together in groups would mirror the experiences we would soon be involved with in the "real world." My group was formed based on geography — we all happened to live in the same apartment complex. By fluke, we also brought a complementary skill set to the table. Scott Sarjent was a lawyer; Doug Bradley had completed a mathematics degree; Chris Andersen had an economics background; and I had just graduated with a B.Sc. in biochemistry. Shelly Ackerman could bake.

Actually, Shelly had also graduated from McGill with a combined degree in business and psychology. Early on, however, she told the group that she felt intimidated by the rest of us. She said her contribution would be to feed us — that was her strength. In return, we'd help her get through Western. At first we thought she was joking, but very quickly her apartment became our preferred destination as we were always greeted by the fresh scent of baked goods when we arrived. Shelly needn't have worried though. She was an integral part of the group, and when we departed from her suggestions, it was usually at our own risk.

Western's primary method of instruction in the MBA program was the case study. Each day our various courses provided three cases that had to be analyzed for the next lesson. Our class consisted of about 60 people sitting in a three-tiered, horseshoe-shaped room. During each class, open discussion was encouraged — how to solve each case and how we would have addressed the real world issues we'd read about. Occasionally, we had to make individual presentations to the rest of the class. Typically, we didn't know until the day of the class who would be chosen to present. One day it was Greg Lennon's turn in the barrel.

Greg had played on the varsity soccer team at McMaster University, and he was a very good looking guy. He oozed charm and was very eloquent. He was quite popular with the women on campus.

The case we were analyzing had to do with the fate of a tanker ship named the Cynthia — did the economics favour the refurbishment of the ship, or should it have been scrapped? As you can imagine, there were a lot of nuanced remarks about Cynthia's body and the like, and the class was in a fairly spirited mood. Greg got up in the middle of the horseshoe to present his recommendations.

As he spoke, his words were like music; there was a rhythm to them and the class was enraptured. But as we listened to what he was actually saying, it became pretty clear that there wasn't much "meat on the bone." He was basically talking gibberish. We all started looking around at each other, and there were more than a few of us stifling grins. Suddenly he stopped.

"I know what you're all thinking," he said. "We all have unique talents and strengths. Some of you are great at math. Some of you can write with an ease that I can only dream about. Some of you are brilliant lawyers, scientists, and artists. Well, I have a strength too. My strength is BULLSHITTING."

The room erupted. When the laughter subsided, he resumed his "analysis" as if nothing had happened. The last I knew, Greg "What, me bullshit?" Lennon (as he came to be known from that point onward) was a senior vice president at a major Canadian bank.

Several years later, I was working at Delta Projects. I had just started and was in a temporary office as my regular digs were prepared. It was late in the day, and I was on the phone making plans for the weekend. I was leaning back in my chair with my feet up on the desk when I saw a blonde vision walk by my door. I literally fell off my chair.

I found out later that her name was Barbara Brown. Barbara worked in the Accounting Department, and for some reason her desk was the most popular in the company — no wonder in an office comprised of 80% male engineers.

A year or so later, I became a member of the social committee at the company. The committee had been having a hard time attracting new members and even participants for many of the planned activities, and they asked me to come up with a way of increasing both.

I went to see Barbara. I asked her if she would be willing to serve on the committee. She seemed suspicious. "Why are you asking?" she said.

"Because I think you could make a valuable contribution," I replied. "We need better participation and I think you could help."

"Why — because of my looks?" she asked.

"Not entirely," I lied. "But we all have our strengths and you can't tell me you've never played to yours."

She thought about what I said for a bit and, fortunately, she laughed knowingly. Barbara joined the social committee, and our participation rates soared.

So here's what I learned: We all have our unique strengths. Identify what yours are, and don't be embarrassed or hesitant to use the gifts you've been given to your advantage. Just use them wisely and for good.

25. Sometimes You Have to Do It Yourself

If you see a snake, just kill it. Don't appoint a committee on snakes.

Ross Perot

You might say I'm a bit of a sports junkie. I can watch almost any competition — athletic or otherwise — and have, throughout the years. Perhaps my lowest point was the afternoon I spent watching darts on television, during which I actually developed a rooting interest in one of the competitors. My home office is decorated with every piece of Montreal Canadiens memorabilia imaginable, from sticks to pucks, sweaters, pictures, and various trinkets emblazoned with my team's logo — either purchased or received as gifts over the years.

I enjoy participating as well. These days, my interests tend more toward individual activities — table tennis, golf, and hiking. I really enjoyed team sports when I was younger, but at a certain point in life, the ease with which you could collect a group of people to play the team sports seems to diminish. As lives become more complicated by family, career, and other obligations, the opportunities to compete in team-based pursuits are outweighed by more serious requirements.

Several years ago I did, however, get to live out one of every father's fantasies. I actually had the opportunity to play on a sports team with one of my children. I was working at Hyundai, and my daughter Rachelle interned for the summer as a service rep, fielding customer calls. Hyundai had a co-ed slo-pitch baseball team, and they were desperate for participants. I was too old by two decades to make a meaningful contribution, and Rachelle's athletic talents leaned in a direction other than baseball. Nevertheless, every week the two of us were out on the field playing catch like a scene out of the movie *Field of Dreams*. It's a summer memory that I will treasure always.

When I was younger, I did consider myself somewhat of a jock. In high school I played almost every team sport imaginable. But my favourite, by far, was football. Not real football, of course — I'd have to be nuts to play that — but the flag football version of the game that kept our brains intact. I played quarterback on offence and defensive back on defence.

There were three elementary schools that fed into my high school — Miller (my school), Laurentide, and Cedar Croft. Laurentide didn't have much of a reputation for athletics, but there was a pretty fierce competition between the Miller guys and the Cedar Croft guys, especially in football.

My next-door neighbour, Alan Krukin, who played on my team, was known as "Big Al." Actually, he was known as Big Al only by himself — it was a self-proclaimed moniker, and he wasn't even all that big. One day, Madame Ardouin, our homeroom French teacher, who had never uttered a single word in English for the entire year, was handing out the results of one of our exams. When she returned Al's exam, we realized she actually had a sense of humour. Beneath the spot where he had proclaimed his name to be Big Al, she had replied, in red ink and perfect English, "Little Marks."

Anyway, Big Al and I were on the Miller team and we were playing the season-ending grudge match between Cedar Croft and Miller. The score was tied and it was getting dark, so we decided, as we had done many times before, to end the game "last touchdown wins." Cedar Croft had the ball deep in their half of the field. It was their last down before they would have to kick. Big Al was the defensive back on the other side of the field from me. We had been playing man-to-man defence for the series, but on this particular play we decided to change up and play zone — we would each cover a part of the field that a receiver would come into rather than being assigned a specific player to guard. We thought that by mixing things up, we would mix them up, but it backfired.

Their receiver split our zone as the ball was thrown. I could have easily knocked down the pass. Big Al could have easily knocked down the pass. He thought I had it. I thought he had it. We both froze. The ball sailed over our heads before we could recover. As the winning touchdown was scored, he looked at me and I looked at him. We lost the game and the season series.

So here's what I learned: Throughout your career, you will likely be assigned tasks as part of a team. Sometimes the communications on teams is less than perfect and responsibilities are not adequately defined. Try to ensure there is clarity about who is going to do what. If that's not possible and if the end result is important to you or to the success of your team's efforts, do it yourself, even if you duplicate the effort. It beats the results that occur when nobody takes action and everyone points fingers.

26. Sometimes You Should Trust Your Gut

Trust your hunches ... Hunches are usually based on facts filed away just below the conscious level.

Dr. Joyce Brothers

I've taken a number of personality profile tests throughout my career to better understand my character, how I operate, and what my needs and preferences are. In all of these profiles, I score very high in logical thinking and reasoning. Maybe my science background has something to do with it, but I tend to be very skeptical of claims that are not tangible and can't be backed up by something that I can feel, see, hear, or otherwise sense. Yet over the course of my career, there have been times when I have come across "gut feelings" or phenomena I haven't been able to reason out.

I worked with Angie Lake at Stone & Webster. I originally hired her as a temporary replacement for someone in the department who had travelled to Europe on an extended vacation. She had graduated from the psychology program at York University. She was in the process of pursuing her Human Resources accreditation at night, but she had never worked in the field. I liked her when she interviewed; she just wanted a "foot in the door." I figured the decision was pretty low risk as the incumbent would only be away for a month, so I decided to hire her for that period. Within about a week in the job, Angie made it pretty clear that she was head and shoulders better than our permanent employee. When he returned from Europe, I persuaded the company President to bump up the head count in my department by one so that we could bring Angie on full time.

Unfortunately, the additional head count didn't last more than a year. The company experienced a downturn in project work and I was asked to downsize by one. Angie stayed.

Along with her skills in the Human Resources area, Angie claimed to have some extra-sensory abilities. She believed in advice from seers and fortune tellers, and she claimed she could sense when she was about to receive a call before her phone would ring. "Yeah, I knew that was going to happen," she would often say. Of course, these kinds of claims were exactly the sort that would make me roll my eyes and think she was a little loopy. And I would chide her about her "abilities" on a regular basis. One day I asked her to prove it.

My kids had a game called *Candyland*. The game came with a set of cards with five different colours. There were thirty cards in the set that I brought in to work. Angie claimed that she could determine the colour of each card by "feeling" the flip side and sensing heat patterns. I, of course, knew she was batty.

I designed what is known as a double-blind experiment — she wouldn't know, nor would I, what the cards were before they were displayed. She would do her "touchy-feely thing," and I would reveal the card to both of us after each guess and track her progress. She had a one in five chance of randomly guessing the colours; that might indicate a reasonable score of 6 out of 30.

We ran the experiment. Angie scored 25. She beamed and I blanched. I checked the cards for bent edges, markings, transparency, and the like. I couldn't find anything unusual. I thought maybe she had an accomplice who somehow — I didn't know how — fed her information. I told her that we would switch places, so I could see what she was seeing, and run it again. That time she scored 28 out of 30. To this day I don't know how she did it; my logical brain will still not allow me to believe that I wasn't duped. Angie eventually left us, rising to become the Human Resources Director at a major office-supply company. I'm sure that somehow her powers have helped.

When we were originally looking to hire a nanny for our eldest daughter, Rachelle, we placed an advertisement in the local newspaper. Elaine and I immediately realized our mistake. The phone rang the entire weekend, dozens of people claiming to have all kinds of experience raising kids. For those who seemed reasonable, we set up interviews. Our interviewees had a 90% no-show rate, and of those who did come to our home, there wasn't one I would have even considered hiring. We were quite depressed. Elaine suggested placing another ad — but in our local community paper. I thought that the *Liberal*, as the paper was called, was only used for wrapping fish, but we were desperate.

We received one call from a woman named Betty Evans. Betty lived within a ten-minute walk from us. We arranged for her to come over to talk. When she came in, she immediately asked whether she could hold the baby. This impressed us. And when Elaine gave over our nine-month-old precious bundle to Betty, Rachelle looked into her eyes and smiled. Now in retrospect, it may have been gas, but Elaine and I took this as a sign. Betty was the only candidate to apply from an obscure ad in an obscure newspaper, and our kid smiled. We hired her.

Betty not only helped to raise Rachelle, but Natalie and Jackie as well. And she remains a part of our family over twenty years later, now caring for my elderly mother. We made one of the best decisions of our lives that day on criteria that, to this day, I can't explain.

Several years later, I was having lunch with an actuary who was a consultant on Stone & Webster's pension plan. An old joke says that an actuary is a guy who flunked the accountant's personality test, but in truth these people are incredibly bright mathematicians who deal

Lessons Learned

with data and logic all day. We got around to talking about outside interests, and he said he was a skydiver. I was incredulous. "You're kidding," I said. "You're an actuary and you choose a risky activity like skydiving for your fun?"

"Actually," he said, "I've looked at all of the statistics, and skydiving has one of the lowest rates of mortality of all sporting activities."

Amazing. A decision made on purely rational and thoughtful analysis that I consider battier than Angie's card trick display or our rationale for choosing our kids' nanny.

So here's what I learned: I can't tell you when or how, but sometimes you will just know in your gut when a decision you make about your career or about a situation at work feels right. I'm not saying that you should disregard logical analysis — I would never say that. But sometimes the right answer lies with your gut.

27. Sometimes You Have to Move

If you treat men the way they are, you never improve them. If you treat them the way you want them to be, you do.

Johann Wolfgang Von Goethe

I'm not a big school reunion guy. Since graduation, I've attended a grand total of one. Not that there haven't been opportunities. After all, my high school, Saint Laurent High, has had a few; and my undergrad, McGill, has one for my graduating class every five years, as does Western's Business School, Ivey. I succumbed once, going to the reunion 15 years after I left Western.

Everyone was very affable, but after the three-day weekend, I realized there was a reason I hadn't kept in touch with most of my class — we had very little in common. And regardless of where we all ended up, everyone seemed to revert to where they had been 15 years previously — the jocks were still the jocks, the nerds the nerds, and the clowns the clowns. It was like we hadn't left, or maybe it had just seemed that way to me because that's how I viewed them and how they viewed me. Sometimes it's like that in the "real world" as well.

When I worked at Petro-Canada, I was hired as a Procedures Analyst, but the major focus of my job was writing administrative policies. We had two secretaries in the department as well as forms designers and several other analysts. Abigail Fech (pronounced like the dog's command) was one such analyst.

Abby and I became close friends in the time I was there. We always joked that one day we would start up our own consulting firm. I suggested the name, "Far-Feched." She laughed at my stupid jokes, basis enough for a friendship, as far as I'm concerned.

Abby started her career as one of the two department secretaries. At the time she was hired, she was a high school graduate and was pursuing her university studies at night. Upon graduation, she was moved into the Analyst role that I also came to occupy. But Abby never felt truly comfortable — not because she didn't like the work or the group, but because she felt that the rest of the organization saw and treated her as if she were still the secretary of the department. It was as though she were attending a perpetual school reunion where everyone viewed her as she was when she first started.

Abby eventually left to join another major oil company, and she went on to become quite successful within the "oil patch." Unfortunately, she felt she had to leave to get the recognition she deserved from the rest of the company.

Every year, most organizations assess their compensation situation by participating in industry-wide or geographical salary surveys. These surveys help to determine where a company's salaries stand in relation to the competition and to the local community.

Most compensation analysis is based on the concept of "compa-ratios." That's the ratio of where a salary fits within an employee's pay grade. Over time, however, I had developed a number of different ratios that I looked at when analyzing compensation data, including something I dubbed the "problem ratio." Without getting into too much detail, the problem ratio is a way of looking at who in the organization is underpaid — not just in relation to the market, but to certain jobs that are "hot" at the time of the survey. The problem ratio would identify the employees most susceptible to being poached by competitors.

At one client's company, I ranked the staff in order of the problem ratios. Of the employees in the top ten, eight had been promoted to their positions from within the organization. The company had recognized their abilities to the extent that they had been promoted, but their salaries had not kept pace with the market over time.

Part of this phenomenon was cultural. At this company you had to start at the bottom and prove yourself worthy of your salary over time. The problem they had, like most organizations, was that the review process in which salaries were determined only provided a finite amount of money to spread around to everyone. That included those in most need, so they were constantly playing catch-up with the people they had promoted. In many cases, the company wasn't able to get the salaries up to market rates. You can guess what happened in at least some of these cases: the competition found a source of trained and qualified candidates who were underpaid in relation to the market.

If you look at organizations who operate by the "show me first and I'll pay you later" model, there is often an underlying assumption. We'll promote you, but we're not entirely sure that you're not — nor will you ever not be — what you were previously. Sort of like Abby's perpetual school reunion.

So here's what I learned: If in your career you find yourself in a position in which you feel underappreciated, sometimes – not always, but sometimes — you just have to move. It's amazing how much more recognized some people become after they leave the organization they're with. Sad but true.

Try to work for an outfit that not only allows you to grow and develop, but also doesn't treat you as if you haven't.

28. We Should All Get Along (Or Not)

The single biggest problem in communication is the illusion that it has taken place.

George Bernard Shaw

I have never been a smoker, with the exception of that one time I smoked a cigar on the night of my last exam at Western. My mouth tasted like road dirt for a week, and I haven't had the urge since. Needless to say, I am not a fan of smoking or of smokers who practice their habit in my vicinity. Despite that stance, I believe we lost something very valuable when we banned smoking in the workplace.

When I began my career, many people would smoke at their desks or in their offices. This began to change as people like me complained about foul air and concerns regarding the effects of second-hand smoke became routine. As a result, companies moved toward establishing smoking areas within their buildings and banning the habit at personal work spaces. These "smoking rooms" were typically closed off and ventilated, and they were the essence of democracy. Smokers from all levels, all departments, and all backgrounds would congregate. Without the normal barriers that a typical organization erects, communication — real communication — would naturally ensue. And then we banned smoking rooms.

As the head of Human Resources, I worked for many organizations that looked to my groups to organize social functions. For years I resisted for two reasons: First, as an introvert, social gatherings tend to leave me slightly cold. And second, I wanted my groups to be considered the professionals that I knew we were, not "fluffy" people who organized Christmas parties. Over time, though, my hardline stance moderated as I began to see the value in groups of people getting together at a human level without barriers. I saw these functions as a replacement for the "smoker's clubs." I figured the more the opportunity to meet outside of the work environment, the better the health of the group. I think I was right, but only to an extent.

Camaraderie and congeniality within organizations and within subgroups of organizations are nice. However, history is full of examples of groups of people who didn't get along but nevertheless achieved greatness. The Oakland Athletics baseball team of the mid 1970s won three World Series championships in a row. They were a great team — arguably one of the best of all time. And they hated each other. But their animosity never led to them to stop communicating.

At one company I worked at, two of the people in my department were Alice Long and Brenda Cates. Alice was a gregarious extravert; she loved to chat with a variety of people from around the company. Brenda was much quieter and quite introverted. I liked and respected them both. But together, they were like oil and water. The communication within our group suffered — they would barely talk to each other. As a result, our performance was not optimal. Not because we didn't like each other, but because we didn't communicate effectively.

Alice ultimately left us to join another firm as their head of Human Resources. Brenda stayed and assumed my role after I left. They were both accomplished professionals, but the performance of our department improved only after they were separated.

During this time, Elaine was working as a Project Manager on a clinical trial for a major pharmaceutical company. Her project involved a variety of people at multiple levels, both temporary and permanent staff. Her project came in on time and under budget. As a reward, and to provide an incentive to their other project groups, the company decided to send all of the team and their spouses or partners on a three-day trip to Arizona. We had a blast. The project staff would meet in the hotel pool once daily to discuss business. Other than that, we were all free to organize group outings, play golf, tour the Grand Canyon, or do whatever else we wanted.

I came back to work very excited and told my group all about what Elaine's company had done. I suggested we might try something similar for our project teams, but the reception I received was less than enthusiastic. Brenda told me that the thought of socializing with our group, regardless of the location, would hardly be an incentive for her. I believe her words were, "I would rather have a root canal."

So here's what I learned: Over the course of your career, you will be involved in many groups or teams. It's nice when everyone in these groups gets along, but it's essential that everyone in the group communicates. Social functions, either formal or informal, may help to some extent — but it's unlikely you'll get everyone involved, and in some cases the event may actually backfire. It's better to set up opportunities for the group to communicate, sort of a "smokers' club" for everyone. If you are in charge of the group, monitor their communication rather than their friendships. That's what matters most.

29. Don't Be Mean to an End

There are two kinds of coaches. The kind that have just been fired and the kind that are going to get fired.

Bum Phillips

Did I mention that I'm a huge fan of the Montreal Canadiens? The team's success over the years has been unparalleled in the hockey world, but as of late, my team has been experiencing a difficult stretch. The Canadiens' fan base is very passionate — and very impatient. Cries of "fire the coach!" ring out after losing streaks of five games or so. I'm sensitive to those calls. First, firing someone is not so easy. Second, when you fire the coach, you fire the coach's wife, his kids, and his extended family. There are other people affected by those firing decisions.

I've worked in the Human Resources field for over thirty years. When I tell people what I do, many of them say something to the effect of, "Oh, you're the guy who hires and fires people." No, I'm not.

In fact over the course of thirty years, I have fired a grand total of two people. I'll make a distinction: I've worked for organizations that have let people go for a variety of reasons, but in almost every case these decisions were made for reasons other than incompetence or inappropriate behaviour. In almost every case, there was a political agenda, an interpersonal conflict between boss and subordinate, or the economic necessity to reduce the size of the organization. Let me tell you about the other two cases.

Robert Ham (not his real name) was a technician in our Information Technology department. In his role, he had access to all of the company's user accounts and could access all of the data stored on the company's servers. He was excellent at his job and was well respected in the organization, but Robert had a soft spot for one of the company's administrative assistants.

It was performance review time and Ken Fields, our Finance Manager, had completed the reviews for his department and stored them in his folder on the company's system. One of Ken's employees had a running feud with the admin assistant Robert was trying to impress, so Robert got access to that employee's review, and he "shared" it with the assistant.

I, along with an assistant in our department, conducted a thorough investigation. We interviewed all of the parties and met with Robert last. To his credit, he didn't deny any part of the story. He apologized for his indiscretion and lack of judgement and said he would never do it again. In the end, we decided that his behaviour had crossed the line where second chances were not possible. His behaviour was wrong on so many levels. He had breached the security of the system he was in charge of maintaining, and he'd done it for purely personal reasons. We fired him for it.

Brian Johnson (not his real name) was a Warranty Advisor responsible for the dealer network; he took calls relating to the warranties on the company's products. His position was one of six such jobs in the company. His group serviced dealers from all across the country, and as such they required staff to be present before most of the rest of the company arrived and after most staff had left for the day. The department set up a rotating shift schedule so that one member of the department arrived at 7 a.m. to service the Atlantic dealers, and one stayed late until 7 p.m. to service the Pacific dealers. Brian usually volunteered for the late shift, and the rest of the department staff was very happy he did.

The company's phone system could produce reports of the number of calls handled, when they were received, and how long each call lasted. But the primary measure of performance of the warranty group was the volume of calls handled by each Advisor. Brian's call volume was always at or near the top of the pack, but something felt wrong to Brian's supervisor. Whenever the supervisor passed by Brian's cubicle, Brian was either away from his desk or doing something other than handling dealer calls. So he asked the IT group to pull the department phone records for the previous three months. Brian's volume was acceptable. The supervisor then asked for secondary reports to be produced — the call durations and when the calls were received.

What he uncovered was a pattern of performance that was brilliant, if only for its ingenuity. Eighty percent of Brian's calls were received between 6 and 7 p.m., after the rest of the department had left. Nearly all of the calls came from relatively few phone numbers. Brian would either have a friend call in to the warranty line and hang up 30 seconds later, or he would use his own cell phone to make the calls himself.

Again we investigated. This time Brian denied any wrongdoing. But the evidence against him over a three-month period was so overwhelming that we fired him. He had been stealing — the company's time. Brian threatened to sue for wrongful dismissal. In turn, we threatened to take him to court for theft. I haven't heard from him since.

Wrongful dismissal is a concept in law whereby a company terminates an employee without proper legal reason and without providing adequate payment for the loss of employment. Throughout my career, I fought for proper compensation for all of the staff that we terminated, and it has worked — I have been in court defending the companies I worked for only once. And that case was thrown out by the judge.

So here's what I learned: At some point in your career you may be in a position where you must let someone go from the organization you represent. If it's your decision solely, do so only as a last resort — either for some form of egregious behaviour or for incompetence. If you are instructed to do so by someone else, do it with as much compassion as possible. In all cases, treat the person with respect, and provide the proper compensation for your decision.

Firing someone is difficult on everyone, you included. Doing so improperly will affect your reputation as much as that of the person you're terminating. Others are watching you, and how you treat someone as they leave is as important as how you treat them when they're with you.

30. Humour is a Very Serious Thing

He who laughs, lasts.

Dr. Robert Anthony

I took Latin in high school. I was one of the six idiots who voluntarily chose Miss Laow's Grade 9 Latin class as an elective — and all six of us gave up the ghost after one year, a move that effectively put an end to the instruction of that language in our school. Still, that year of study has actually helped me over time. First, it has been a tremendous aid in figuring out the derivation of words I don't understand. And second, because I have a number of friends who are lawyers whose training includes a sprinkling of Latin phrases, I can actually follow some of their obscure references.

Tim Morris was a manager in our Marketing department. He was an engineer by training and had worked for a number of years with one of the largest utility companies in Canada. We had hired him to help build up our power business mostly because of his contacts: those he had developed at his previous company and with other potential clients, primarily in Ontario. Tim could talk — boy could he talk. When Tim came into my office for a five minute conversation, I knew I was in for at least half an hour.

Bob Barnes was Tim's counterpart in Marketing, but he was on the process side of the business. His role was to develop similar client relationships in the development of refinery and gas processing projects with the likes of Petro-Canada, Imperial Oil, and others. Bob was a classically trained engineer from England — a true gentleman, and a very funny guy. Apparently as part of his classical schooling, he too had to learn Latin.

It was part of both Bob and Tim's role to assist in developing the commercial terms of the contracts that we entered into with their clients. The primary responsibility for the creation of these contracts rested with Gerald Caruthers, our Corporate Counsel. In appearance, Gerald was the antithesis to Bob Barnes. He had grown up in the blue-collar section of Steeltown — Hamilton, Ontario. If Bob would be considered a British "dandy," Gerald looked like he had come directly off of the football field and into his office. But he was also a great lawyer with a wickedly dry sense of humour.

One day, Gerald and Bob were in the process of putting together the contract for a project that Bob had brought in to the company. It was a complex deal, and the negotiations with the client had been quite challenging, but both parties had finally come to a verbal agreement. They were exchanging emails about the wording of the contract when Bob ended one of his messages with: "Be careful. *Vox audita perit littera scripta manet.*"

Gerald picked up the phone and asked Bob to come into his office.

When Bob arrived, Gerald said to him, "You know, I'm a lawyer and I know lots of Latin expressions. But buddy, you've got me with this one. What are you talking about?"

"Really?" Bob asked. "I thought you'd know that one. It means, 'The spoken word perishes, but the written word goes on forever.'"

Gerald thought for a moment, leaned back in his chair, and said, "You know, Bob, I'm not so sure that's right. Just before you came, I had your counterpart, Mr. Morris, in here. I can assure you — in his case, the spoken word goes on forever."

It was one of the best one-liners I have ever come across in my career.

Things just sound so much more impressive in Latin. Who can forget the words of Robin Williams's character in the film *Dead Poets Society*, exhorting his charges to *carpe diem*? Seize the day.

I play a lot of poker. After a "bad beat" — a hand in which the loser should have won but the cards dictated otherwise — one of the most common expressions you tend to hear around a table is "that's poker." Really?

Wouldn't the Latin expression used in the legal world *res ipsa loquitur*, the thing speaks for itself, sound much more impressive? (In the common vernacular it means, "it is what it is." Or, "that's poker.") Okay, maybe not around a bunch of beer swilling, cigar smoking guys, but you get my drift.

I attended McGill. Our school motto was *Grandescunt aucta labore* (by work, all things increase and grow). Then I attended graduate school at Western where it is *Veritas et utilitas* (truth and usefulness). Awesome.

Elaine and Rachelle attended Queen's: *Sapientia et doctrina stabilitas* (wisdom and knowledge shall be the stability of thy times).

Jackie is at Laurier: *Veritas omnia vincit* (truth conquers all).

And Natalie is at McMaster: *Ta panta en Christoi synesteken* (In Christ all things hold together). Wait ... that's Greek not Latin. Never mind.

So here's what I learned: At a minimum, know your school's motto — and live it. These mottos are actually quite inspiring. You may also want to learn a few additional Latin phrases. They tend to make people, especially lawyers, think you're intelligent, if only slightly nerdy.

And never underestimate the value of humour in your career. It not only adds to the enjoyment of everyone's day, but if you come up with a great line, it will be remembered long after most other things you say and do are forgotten.

31. Fifteen Minutes of Fame

I am not concerned that I am not known, I seek to be worthy to be known.

Confucius

Andy Warhol once said, "In the future, everyone will be world famous for 15 minutes." I was almost world famous for 15 minutes, if the world means Canada and famous means being on television. Today, that describes almost any reality TV show, but back in the 1970s, it was fairly rare.

Three of my buddies — Jerry Molnar, Lorne Erdile, Zsolt Kekesi — and I made up our high school *Reach for the Top* team. *Reach for the Top* was a quiz show produced by local CBC affiliates across Canada. It was originally created in the late 1950s to showcase the "best and brightest" students from across the country. Apparently when the Russians launched Sputnik into orbit in 1957, we felt the need to demonstrate we hadn't fallen behind in our production of people capable of matching them. Supposedly, the ability to answer a series of trivia questions equated "rocket science."

Saint Laurent High was the smallest school in the city of Montreal, and we were actually its last graduating class. We weren't supposed to have a team that year, but one of the other schools decided not to enter and we became the 32nd and final entry. Our school had never passed the second round, and expectations on us were not much greater. But we won our first game and continued to win — eventually all the way to the Quebec finals. There, we set the single game record for most points scored in the history of the show. In doing so, we qualified for the Canadian championships.

The national finals were held in Ottawa, where we also continued to win — all the way to the championship game, in which we faced a team from Barrhead, Alberta. Our semi-final was played the night before the final game. Having won the semis, we were guaranteed a trip to Europe — if we won the final, we went to Paris; if we lost, to London. With a trip in hand, we partied that night. The team from Alberta played their semi-final the same day as the final game, but in the morning. They didn't party when we did; they studied. We got killed.

The nationals, which were filmed over the course of a week, were aired throughout the summer, and we were sworn to secrecy regarding the result. The show had quite a loyal following, and as each game in our road to the final game aired, the four of us became local celebrities. I was recognized on the street a number of times, and to say it didn't go to my head would not be completely accurate.

I was still flying high the following year when I attended Vanier College in Montreal. Vanier is a CEGEP and, in the Quebec system, a bridge between high school and university. I attended for two years prior to entering McGill. I was recognized in the halls of Vanier as well. My head continued to swell — until I flunked my introductory physics class for not completing assignments. As painful as that experience was, it brought me thudding back to reality. It was a wake-up call I badly needed.

We received our runner-up prize the following spring break. The CBC, through an outfit called the Heritage Society of Canada, arranged for the four of us to spend a week in London. The trip was all-expenses paid, including food and lodging, and there was a small stipend provided for additional spending. Prior to our departure, the four of us decided to purchase T-shirts emblazoned with "Canada" across the front and different numbers on the back. We wore these shirts throughout the week, and we were stopped many times by locals asking if we were from Canada (insightful lot) and what team we represented. My buddy Zsolt, who was by far the best "BSer" of all of us, would come up with a novel answer each time the question was asked. Far be it for us to have told the truth — we were a team comprising the second-best book nerds in all the country.

We were accompanied on our trip by a chaperone, a producer from the CBC. However, after settling in, we saw him on only a couple of other occasions throughout the week — once to play poker in his hotel room and a second time in front of Buckingham Palace where the four of us were filmed by a local film crew as we watched the changing of the guard. The footage was to be aired the following summer during that year's *Reach for the Top* finals, but I don't think our faces ever made it back to the screen.

So we were four 19-year-old guys left mostly to our own devices in London. There were locations that they had us scheduled to see, but as you can imagine, many of the sights we chose to witness were the local establishments, and the activity we were most interested in was sampling the liquid refreshments therein.

One evening, we were provided with tickets to see a relatively new performer play at a small club in the city. We had a basic idea of who he was — he had an album that had been released and a couple of the songs had gotten some airtime back home. But we decided that because he wasn't sufficiently famous, we would instead visit another pub that we hadn't yet frequented a couple of blocks away from our hotel. As a result we missed the opportunity to see an up-and-coming talent just as he was beginning to perfect his stage performances in front of small, intimate crowds. His name was Elton John.

So here's what I learned: Maybe in the course of your career you'll get your 15 minutes of fame. Don't let it get to your head. First, it won't last. Second, it's not important. What matters is your values. Know them and live by them. You'll be far happier if you do.

In our society today, where fame has been cheapened by reality television and style seems to triumph over substance, when you decide to invest your time and choose a course of action to follow, do so wisely. Choose the quality of ideas, beliefs, values, and even art based on what is being said, written, or performed rather than by who is doing the speaking, the writing, or the performing. Many famous people today won't be around nearly as long as the "unknown" we chose to miss that night in London.

32. Don't Leave for Money; Don't Stay Out of Fear

He that is of the opinion money will do everything may well be suspected of doing everything for money.

Benjamin Franklin

I had been working with Stone & Webster for about seven years when I was approached by a headhunter to interview for a position that she was trying to fill. I wasn't really interested, but I hadn't been interviewed since I joined the company, and I felt I needed the practice — just in case. So I agreed to see her. I had anticipated most of her questions and talked about my background, my accomplishments, and how I thought I could help her client. Then she asked me a question I wasn't prepared for. I had assumed she would ask why I would consider leaving Stone & Webster — a fairly routine question aimed at uncovering what aspects of the position I didn't care for. Instead she asked. "Why have you stayed in the same company for seven years?"

To me, this question was every bit as valid — sort of the flip side to what I'd thought she would ask — but I just hadn't heard it before. After the interview, and though I still wasn't interested in the position, her question got me to thinking. *Why had I stayed?* I would get my answer a little while later.

Alan Webber, the founder and first editor of *Fast Company* magazine, delivered a talk to the Ivey Business School, and alumni of the school were invited to participate remotely. I attended via conference call. Alan's topic was "How Companies Can Win the War for Talent," and he based his talk on a research study that was conducted by McKinsey & Company, a large consulting firm specializing in corporate strategy. McKinsey's findings suggested that there were four viable strategies that a firm could use to attract the best and the brightest:

1) Save the World.

This strategy involves selling and living the message that this company is involved in activities that will better the human race, or our local community — however you define it.

2) We Will Make You Fabulously Wealthy.

This strategy, typically for high tech start-ups, involves selling and living the message that you can work 20 hours a day, for however long you last, but that at the end of your tenure, you will be set for life financially.

3) Work–Life Balance.

This strategy involves selling and living the message that the world is a crazy place — you can work 24 hours a day and still not accomplish all you need to. But work for us, and you will actually get home at a normal time and have a normal family life, and you might even get to know your kids' teachers' names.

4) The Seal of Approval on Your Resume.

This strategy involves selling and living the message that if you work for us, even if you leave after a period of time, at the end of your career you can look back and realize that your time here was the most valuable and meaningful learning experience you had.

As the head of HR, I reflected on Webber's talk from the employer perspective — how could we use these concepts to differentiate what we should offer in order to attract people to our company? It also struck me that, if flipped, these strategies were also legitimate reasons for people — myself included — to stay with their firms. If I couldn't honestly say that at least one of these applied to my current situation, it was time for me to consider leaving. When I looked back to the headhunter's interview question, the reason I had stayed was that I believed I was still learning and growing my craft — Webber's strategy number four.

I have had eight jobs since graduation and I left each of them for the following reasons:

1) The Calgary Herald. I felt restricted to one aspect of the HR function and was given the opportunity at another company to broaden my scope.

2) Delta Projects. Alberta's economy went into recession after the Federal National Energy Program was announced. Delta lost projects and had to downsize to survive. I was the last layoff, but otherwise I would have stayed.

3) Petro-Canada. The company head office was relocating from Toronto to Calgary. Had I been single, I would have moved back, but Elaine had a career in Toronto, and we both thought it would be easier for me to find something in the East than she could in the West.

4) National Cheese. National was a small family-run business. After setting up their HR department, I felt there was nowhere to go. As much as I loved the people and the atmosphere, without being a family member, I felt my options were limited.

5) Hyundai (the first time). I felt stifled by the culture, and when I was asked to do some things that crossed a moral line for me, I felt I had to leave.

Lessons Learned

6) Stone & Webster. The company had been bought out by a construction firm in the States, and the new firm centralized most of the Human Resources decision-making in Louisiana. I no longer felt challenged working there.

7) TGO. I loved the work and the culture but missed the ability to affect meaningful change that, I felt, could only occur by staying with one group for a lengthy stretch.

8) Hyundai (the second time). The culture was still too stifling, and my boss and I had different visions of what mattered from a people perspective.

When I look back on my career, for each position I left (with the exceptions of Delta and Petro-Canada, when I really had no choice), I made the decision because none of Webber's four talent strategies remained — they may have been there at the start, but not by the end. In several cases, I accepted positions with lower salaries in order to join firms where I felt I could learn, contribute, and grow.

When people left the organizations I worked for, as the head of HR, I rarely (if ever) tried to talk them out of it. In their minds, there was a legitimate reason for them to leave. But I would also caution them that leaving for money — which was sometimes the case — would be a mistake ... unless of course they were leaving to become fabulously wealthy and would be set for life financially. There just isn't enough money in moderate pay bumps to make up for the lack of "saving the world," "work–life balance," or "the seal of approval on your resume."

So here's what I learned: When you look for your first job, try to find an organization that delivers on at least one of the four talent strategies. I realize that for your first job, you might not have the luxury — it is far easier to find the right fit, when you have some experience to sell. But once you have been a position for a while, and throughout your career, continue to take stock of your situation on a regular basis. If you find yourself stagnating, don't stay in a position for fear of looking for something new or because you are merely comfortable or complacent. Find a situation that better meets your needs, however you define them. On the other hand, don't leave a company that is meeting your needs solely for more money (unless it will set you for life). It may be trite, but money won't buy you happiness.

Here's a proviso: As your career progresses, certain life situations may dictate that you stay in a position that doesn't meet your needs — family responsibilities, financial constraints, and the like. If that's the case, find something in your life outside of work that will provide the growth, family balance, or community involvement opportunities that you need. That outlet will help both you and your company in the long run.

33. The Power of Money

There are people who have money and people who are rich.

Coco Chanel

After she graduated from Queen's University, our eldest daughter Rachelle moved to Japan to teach English before resuming her academic career. Toward the end of her stay, Elaine and I took advantage of Rachelle's adventure to visit a part of the world we hadn't yet seen. We toured Japan as part of an amazingly accomplished group of professional people before meeting up with Rachelle at the tour's completion.

Cheryl Copman was one member of the group. She was an English teacher from an exclusive private school in New York City, and she had been teaching all of her adult life, including a twenty-year stint at her current school. Cheryl and her husband wanted to take advantage of her spring break to tour Japan. Realizing the 10-day break wouldn't be sufficient, she approached the school principal and told her that she would be taking an additional three days off. Initially the principal agreed, but as the date of the trip approached, she wrote an email to Cheryl saying: "I am hearing that you will be taking some time off next week. Did you discuss this with me?"

Cheryl responded with a beautifully crafted email befitting a career English teacher from an exclusive private school in New York. It could have been interpreted in a number of ways, but one of these ways was clear: "Yes, I did. I am going. Piss off."

As she recounted her story to us over breakfast, Cheryl said that she rarely took time away from work, even when sick, and over her twenty-year employment with the school, she had missed only a handful of days. She was astounded that the principal would raise a three-day absence as an issue under the circumstances. Cheryl went on to say that she and her husband were well off financially, and she was working only for the love of the job. And in this case, she was prepared to accept whatever consequences arose from her decision. Her money allowed her to take a stand.

Lee Trevino was an elite golfer in the 1970s, and he won a number of golf's major championships. Trevino had grown up as a poor kid in southwest Texas and had learned the game of golf on his own. One day he was asked by a reporter how it was that he could look so cool putting at the Masters — one of the game's most important tournaments. How could he withstand the pressure of standing over a putt on the 18th green, knowing that he could win or lose vast earnings in both prize money and endorsements?

Trevino responded by saying, "To me that's not pressure. When I was a kid, I used to hustle golf for $100 a game at municipal courses in Texas. Standing over a putt on the 18th green that would either win or lose a match, and knowing I didn't have the $100 in my pocket to pay off if I missed — that was pressure." Trevino's money allowed him to withstand the demands of the game he loved.

At the end of my second tenure at Hyundai, I was very unhappy. The relationship with my boss, which had begun well five years earlier, had deteriorated significantly over the final two years, to the point where both of us would find it painful to be in the same room together. He was as unhappy with me as I was with him.

At year-end, I was in his office for my annual performance review. I knew that it wasn't going to be a positive experience. I had already anticipated what I would see when he passed his comments across his desk for me to review. Sure enough, his assessment of my performance was universally horrible.

"Do you want to discuss this?" he asked.

"Not really," I replied.

He seemed surprised. "OK. Do you see any of this improving over the next year?" he asked.

"No," I responded.

Again he seemed taken aback. "No? Why not?"

"Because I believe that your assessment of me is based on a complete difference in how we view the world from a people perspective. Your view of my job and what I should be doing is 180 degrees from what I think I should be doing. At this stage in my career, you're not going to change me, and at this stage in your career, I'm not going to change you. I'm realistic enough to know that when the boss and the employee don't see eye-to-eye, the boss wins. There's only one way that this will end, so we might as well end it sooner than later." And very shortly after that discussion he did.

As part of the agreement I had with the company, Hyundai provided me with what is known as "outplacement services." Outplacement is intended to help people find new employment and move on. During one of the first sessions with my outplacement counsellor, I recounted how the employment relationship came to an end. "That was a very courageous stance you took," he said.

I replied: "Not really. My wife and I have paid off our mortgage and put two kids through university, and while we're not rich, we have enough money to live comfortably. If I had said the same thing and taken the same approach earlier in my career when I couldn't have afforded it, maybe that would have been courageous. Or stupid. Or both." In this case, money had allowed me to get out of a situation that I was very unhappy in.

Money means very different things to different people. For some, money simply provides the necessities of life — food, shelter, and clothing. For others, it allows them to buy additional material pleasures and to accumulate assets. For yet others, money represents a way of keeping score in life — a way to determine where they rank in some form of hierarchy. Professional basketball player Kevin Garnett once turned down a contract that would have paid him $23 million per year, saying it was an insult. Others were paid more and he viewed himself to be elite. In his case, the money would have more than paid for necessities and other pleasures.

So here's what I learned: Too often, the pursuit of material gain or a focus on where one stands in relation to others becomes a treadmill that's very difficult to get off. Whatever someone has, at whatever level they're at, it seems never to be enough.

For the wise, money actually buys something much greater — the ability to affect behaviour. The true power of money is the way it allows us to behave in a manner that's true to our values and to perform at a level where fear of failure isn't a factor. Know how much is sufficient for you to live the life you want — with your values intact. Consider getting off the treadmill now and then and enjoy your life to the fullest.

34. Find and Keep the Right Partner

If you want to go quickly, go alone. If you want to go far, go together.

African Proverb

Anna and Ted Farkas had been married for 60 years when my dad passed away at the age of 89. My father came to Canada from Romania in 1947 after World War II. Two years later he was introduced to my mom through a mutual friend when she came to visit Montreal from her native New York City. They were married the following year. It was only later in life that I learned that they got together over my mother's family's objections. After all, they reasoned, why would a native-born American want to marry a "newcomer"? She should want better for herself. Over the next 60 years they would get their answer.

Both my parents worked outside of the home — very unusual for the late 1950s and 1960s. Those were the days of single incomes, and a woman would typically stay at home after the kids would come along. Over the course of their careers, sometimes my mom would earn more than my dad until his next salary increase, and then the situation would reverse until my mom's next pay bump. This alternation went on until almost the day my dad retired. And my parents shared not just their incomes.

I remember being in homeroom class in high school one day, and I'm not sure how, but I let it be known that my father did the laundry in our house.

"How big is your mother?" came a voice from the back of the room.

Not very, in reality — just big enough to be my dad's equal in everything other than physical stature. They were different — but equal.

In 1977, my parents faced a dilemma. The Parti Québécois government headed by René Lévesque had just been elected in Quebec and there was a sense among many English speakers in the province that they would become "second class" citizens. My father, who had lived through the war in Europe and lost his family in the camps, said that once was enough. My parents were determined to leave, but they both had careers. They decided jointly to relocate as soon as either one of them found an equivalent position anywhere in North America. My mother's job offer arrived first, from the Alberta Children's Hospital in Calgary. So they moved out west.

When I started at Delta Projects in Calgary, I was about 25 years old. For some reason, the others in the department were very concerned for my well-being, especially in light of the fact that I wasn't yet married. They had all kinds of suggestions for me — which "meat markets" to frequent, and whom they wanted to set me up with. But I told them not to bother. I knew exactly who I was going to marry.

"Who?" they asked.

"Well, to be fair, I don't know who yet. But I know what. I want someone smart, funny, and with the same values that I have. And she has to be hot," I said.

It wasn't until I returned back east, to Toronto, that I knew who. I met Elaine through a mutual friend. She, like me, had just moved to the city. I had known of her through my friend back in Montreal, and she was a year behind me in the biochemistry program at McGill. We had acknowledged each other as my class ended and hers was beginning.

Lessons Learned

On our first date, she leaned over my plate of food and picked something off before I had a chance to eat it. I thought that was hilarious. When we started to talk, it was very clear she was smart. And over the next few weeks, when we really started to get to know each other, it became clearer that our values were very much in synch. But was she hot?

Years later I was sitting in my office when one of our senior project managers, David Taylor, came in. I had pictures of my three daughters on display on top of a side cabinet. David looked at the pictures then looked back at me. He looked at the pictures again, then back at me. After a few more glances back and forth, he asked, "Are those your daughters?"

"Yes," I replied.

"Wow. Your wife must be gorgeous." Yeah, she was hot.

When we got engaged, we visited a number of jewellers looking for the perfect wedding rings. We found them. They were one half yellow gold, one half white gold, in an interlocking pattern. Two different yet equal halves.

Elaine and I have been married for close to thirty years now. Her career path led her to continue in science, in the clinical research field within the pharmaceutical industry. My path led to Human Resources. Over the course of our careers, at one time or another, she has earned more than me, and I more than her, depending on our employers and our positions.

At one point we faced a career choice similar to the one my parents had. After I moved back east from Calgary, I joined Petro-Canada Products, the refining and distribution branch of the company. In a twist of fate, three years after I joined them and two years after we were married, Petro-Canada Products moved their offices from Toronto to Calgary and offered me a relocation package back to where I had been. We jointly decided to stay in Toronto. We believed it would be easier for me to find another opportunity in the east than for Elaine to find a pharmaceutical job in the west. One month later I joined National Cheese.

So here's what I learned: Life is a journey best taken with a partner with whom you share a mutual respect. Your career will be part of that journey.

Over the years I've known many couples wherein one partner's career path led to the diminishing or elimination of the other's. Often those partnerships fell apart.

If you are faced with a career choice that will impact your partner in this way, make sure that you make your decisions jointly with your mutual best interests fully in mind. In the end, your career is only part of your journey.

35. Find Your Reason

If we have our own "why" of life we shall get along with almost any "how."

Friedrich Nietzsche

My dad died a few years ago, shortly after we threw my parents a party celebrating their 60th wedding anniversary. He died one week shy of the actual date of their diamond anniversary, but shortly after the funeral I was rummaging through their old papers. I uncovered their marriage license, obtained at Montreal's City Hall, and it was dated 60 years to the day he died. He had made it after all.

The eulogy I delivered at his memorial service was the toughest speech I have ever had to make, but writing it was relatively easy. I just retold the stories that he himself had told to me on those rare occasions that he talked about his life before coming to Canada. In the eulogy, I started by quoting the first few lines of the "Serenity Prayer" by Reinhold Niebuhr:

"God grant me the serenity to accept the things I cannot change; courage to change the things I can; and wisdom to know the difference."

My father was a survivor of the Holocaust. For most of my childhood and early adult life, he rarely talked about his experiences during the war. When our youngest daughter, Jackie, was born, however, he decided that he wanted to get his stories on the record so that my children's generation and the generations that follow would never forget what had happened. Following the release of the movie *Schindler's List*, the director, Steven Spielberg set up a foundation to collect the testimony of Holocaust survivors like my dad. My father participated in the project. He told many stories of his life growing up in Eastern Europe, but for me, three of the stories stand out as examples of his serenity, his courage, and his wisdom.

The first took place near the end of the war. He was part of a group of prisoners that was being led on a forced march to deliver a convoy of supplies in support of the German war effort. The convoy was attacked by Russian war planes, and to protect the supplies, the prisoners were ordered to lie on top of the flatbed truck bearing the load — a human shield. They had no choice; they would have had to face either the Russian warplanes or the German guns. As the planes approached, bullets flew past my father's head. He closed his eyes and prepared to die, knowing there was nothing he could do but accept his fate. When he survived, he vowed to live each of his remaining days as if they were a bonus — and he did just that.

The second story took place while he was imprisoned in a concentration camp. The men's and the women's barracks were separated, and he had been assigned to clean the area between the two buildings. There was a strictly enforced "no communication" policy — the prisoners were not allowed to speak. One of the women inside her barracks called to my dad to get a message to her husband. My father remained silent, but the camp Commandant came up to him, pistol pointed at my dad's head, and shouted, "Jew! Why did you talk to that woman?"

My father looked the officer in the eyes and said, "I never said a word." After a standoff that lasted a few seconds but seemed like a few hours, the Commandant lowered his gun and walked away.

Several minutes later, one of the guards came up to my father and said, "That's the first time that I saw him *not* pull the trigger." It was his courage to speak truth to power.

The final story took place on the last day of his imprisonment. My father awoke to the find the camp deserted. Later that day, the Russian troops who had liberated the camp made the prisoners an offer. They told them that the German guards had fled into the surrounding woods. They offered the prisoners guns and told them they had a couple of hours to go out and shoot any of the guards they could find. My dad refused. "No," he said to one of the Russian soldiers, "I have seen too much killing already."

He showed wisdom, to know the difference between right and wrong.

My dad's experiences in the war changed him; I'd suggest it would have changed most people. He viewed life and what was important very differently than he had before. And he viewed death differently, too — he never again feared it, after having cheated it in the camps. To an extent, he passed that on to me. I don't really fear death either.

My maternal grandmother died when I was four years old. I have a very vague recollection of Irene and of running through her small house in Florida with a toy six-shooter attached to a holster around my waist. That's it. Everything else I remember of her is through the stories my mom told me and through old family photographs. And she was the only grandparent I knew; my mother's father died when my mom was a child, and my father's parents were killed in the concentration camps.

My father was seven years older than my mother, and he was born in 1921. In the year 1920, there wasn't one person alive in my family whom I really "knew."

While my ancestors were around then, the fact that I didn't exist in 1920 bothers me not the least. For me, it feels the equivalent of not being around in the time of Julius Caesar.

Elaine and I have three great kids. Perhaps one day they will have their own kids. And their kids will have kids. As I write this, I am 57 years old. There is a chance I will know my kids' kids. The chances of my knowing my kids' kids' kids are none. Barring a miracle of medicine, no one I know will be around in the year 2120. The fact that I won't exist in 2120 (even though my successors will) doesn't scare me any more than my not having been around in 1920.

It's not that some things don't bother me though.

When I was a young adult, I could throw a football far and very fast — 60 yards like a bullet. I could break the fingers of the guys who would catch my passes, and I take a slightly perverse pride in having done so twice.

When Rachelle was born, I had literally never held a baby before. This was not surprising; we were a very small family, and as I have no siblings, I'd had very few opportunities. The neonatal nurse obviously sensed my discomfort as she held out my new daughter for me to hold for the first time.

"You've never held a baby before, have you?" she asked. "It's easy — have you held a football?"

"Sure," I replied.

"OK, then tuck her head in the crux of your elbow, and hold her body along your arm. Just don't spike the kid when you're done." Good advice for life.

So I did. And subsequently I held Natalie and Jackie the same way. All three of them are "slightly" bigger now, and I'll never be able to hold them like that again. And I'll never be able to throw a football that far and fast. These things bother me.

My current passion is table tennis. One day I know I'll no longer be able to play. One day I'll probably not be able to walk up stairs any longer, and I just might soil my pants like I did when I was a baby. That bothers me too. Those things bother me, but they don't scare me.

My dad died at the age of 89. The end was relatively sudden. He suffered a massive heart attack, and he battled for a full day after suffering two more. At one point he turned to his nurse and said, "Tell me honestly. What are my chances of competing in the next Olympics?" Later that day he succumbed.

Up until then he was the primary caregiver to my mother — his wife of sixty years — who suffered from Alzheimer's. He never lost his reason.

That's the only thing that scares me — that someday I might lose my reason for living.

So here's what I learned: Find your reason. Maybe at this point in your life, your career will be it. But understand that your reason may change over time and that's OK. If it does, make sure that you replace it with the one thing that keeps you going so that you never lose your reason for living.

And live each day as if it is a bonus. Because this is all we have.

36. Tell Me a Story

There is no greater agony than bearing an untold story inside you.

Maya Angelou

The stories of the reader or the reader's parent, mentor, or counsellor will likely be even more valuable to you in illustrating the points I have tried to make than the stories in this book. By using my stories as examples and the questions that follow as guides, you will open the door to lessons that resonate at a more personal level.

"But I can't tell stories," some people say. Yet we all do every day — at the dinner table, in the bar, at the water cooler, and virtually everywhere else that we congregate with friends and associates. And people are usually interested. Why? Because the stories are real, they're relevant, they're meaningful, they're natural — and they're ours. You don't have to be Shakespeare to tell a story — there was only one of him. But there are about 7 billion of us.

Engage your audience. Discuss your story with them. Encourage them to ask questions and to share their stories in return.

I have enjoyed telling you my stories. Now have fun telling yours.

1. **You Don't Have to Have It All Figured Out**

    a. Professionally, are you currently working at what you thought you would be doing at this point in your career?

    b. If you are, what has kept you moving along that path? If not, what changed in your interests, your experiences, or your circumstances that led you to where you are now?

    c. Tell me a story that illustrates either why you have stayed on your initial career path or why you switched to a different path.

2. **Your Reputation Precedes You**

    a. Have you ever been in a career situation where a decision that you made ultimately reflected on your reputation, either favourably or unfavourably?

    b. What would have made you change that decision one way or the other?

    c. Tell me a story that illustrates a career situation in which you had to choose a course of action that would have impacted or did impact your reputation.

3. **Communicate Your Priorities**

    a. Of all of your priorities, which is number one?

    b. Have you ever been in a position where you had to choose between what was best for your career and another priority?

    c. Tell me a story that illustrates how you handled a conflict between your priorities in your career and another important facet of your life.

4. **The Importance of Humility**

    a. Give me an example of someone you have come across in your career whom you respected for demonstrating a characteristic that you particularly value.

    b. What was that characteristic, and why is it important to you?

    c. Tell me a story that illustrates how someone you consider a role model in your career demonstrated a characteristic that you particularly value.

5. **You Think You Know but You Don't**

    a. Can you think of an example of a time in your career when you made an assumption about another person and were proven wrong?

    b. To what do you attribute the mistake in the assumption you made?

    c. Tell me a story that illustrates how an assumption you made about another person was ultimately proven wrong.

6. **Learn to Forgive**

    a. Is there a situation in your career when you said or did something that you regret? Or when you didn't say or do something?

    b. If you had a "do over" in that situation, what might you have done differently?

    c. Tell me a story from your career experience that illustrates your forgiveness of either another person or of yourself.

7. Sometimes You Have to Break the Rules

   a. Have you ever had to break a company policy or rule in order to accomplish a goal for your employer?

   b. What were some of the factors you considered in making that decision, and what consequences did you face (or could you have faced) for breaking the rule or policy?

   c. Tell me a story that illustrates a time when you "broke the rules," however you define that idea.

8. Believe in Yourself

   a. Was there ever a time in your career when you doubted your ability to perform a certain job, task, or objective that was put in front of you?

   b. What factors led you to overcome those fears?

   c. Tell me a story that illustrates a time when you ultimately succeeded at a challenge about which you had initial doubts.

9. **Look at the World Differently**

    a. Can you think of a time during your career when you initially failed to accomplish a task yet ultimately succeeded?

    b. Did your attitude or approach play any part in the accomplishment?

    c. Tell me a story that illustrates a time when a shift in your attitude or approach to an issue turned a situation that was difficult for you into a success.

10. **People Are Not Simple**

    a. During your career, have you ever been surprised by someone's reaction to a decision you made that involved them?

    b. If so, what incorrect assumptions that you made about the other person may have played a role in the situation? Did you attempt to discuss the decision with them beforehand?

    c. Tell me a story that illustrates a time in your career when you were taken by surprise by the reaction of another person to a decision you made unilaterally.

11. Loyalty Is Not Dead

    a.   To what organization or person do you consider yourself most loyal?

    b.   What attributes does that organization or person possess that deserve your loyalty?

    c.   Tell me a story that illustrates how your loyalty to an organization or a person may have been tested, what the outcome was, and what you learned.

12. You Don't Owe Your Heart

    a.   Who is the best boss you have ever worked for?

    b.   What attributes did that boss have that made you want to work for and follow him or her?

    c.   Tell me a story that illustrates how your favourite boss acted in a way that inspired you to want to give him or her your full commitment.

13. The World Isn't Entitled to Your Opinion

   a. Have you ever worked for a boss who stifled your growth?

   b. If so, what specifically did he or she do that lessened your development? How did he or she behave toward you that limited your growth?

   c. Tell me a story that illustrates how you or someone you have worked with may have had their development negatively affected by a boss or employer.

14. Don't Lie on Your Resume

   a. Have you ever lied on your resume? Or do you know someone who has?

   b. If so, why did you or they lie? If not, why didn't you feel the need to lie?

   c. Tell me a story that illustrates a time in your career when you or another person may have suffered the consequences of lying or embellishing the truth.

15. Interviews Can Be Challenging

    a.   What is the strangest interview experience you have had or the strangest interview question you have ever had to answer?

    b.   How did you handle the situation or question?

    c.   Tell me a story about the weirdest interview experience you have had in your career, how did you handle it, and what did you learn from it.

16. Learn to Tell a Compelling Story

    a.   What attributes make a story compelling to you?

    b.   Have you ever used a story or stories to help you achieve a goal in your career?

    c.   Tell me a compelling story that illustrates a point. What point are you trying to get across, and how will that story make the point stick in the mind or your audience?

17. Get Comfortable in Front of a Crowd

    a. Have you ever had to overcome the fear of speaking in public?

    b. If so, what techniques did you learn and use to help you speak or present confidently?

    c. Tell me a story about the most effective speech or presentation that you've made during your career and what lessons you learned in making it.

18. Make a List

    a. What are the most important tasks or routines that you have to complete accurately in your present position?

    b. What techniques do you use to ensure that the tasks or routines are completed accurately every time? Do you simply rely on your experience to get it right?

    c. Tell me a story about a critical task that you have had to perform with complete accuracy, what the consequences of failure were to you or other people, and how you ensured you got it right.

19. The Complications of Culture and Language

    a. Have you ever come across a situation in your career where a misunderstanding resulted between you and another person because of differences of language or culture?

    b. How did you overcome those differences to improve your mutual understanding?

    c. Tell me a story that illustrates how you overcame cultural or language differences between you and another person that ultimately improved the relationship or the understanding between you.

20. Just Say Thanks

    a. Have you ever been in a situation where you unintentionally offended someone based on their culture?

    b. If so, what did you learn from the experience?

    c. Tell me a story about a cultural faux-pas that you or someone you know committed and how it affected the relationship with another person.

21. Reward Systems Sometimes Don't Reward

a. Have you ever been disappointed by a salary increase or a bonus that you did not believe reflected your performance?

b. In your view, what may have contributed to your not having received what you thought you should have?

c. Tell me a story that illustrates how a system your employer put in place may have had a negative effect on either your performance or that of the entire organization.

22. Understand Data

a. Have you ever come across an example in your career where an organization or an individual had intuitive beliefs that you questioned?

b. Have you ever had the opportunity to perform analyses that would either back up or disprove those beliefs?

c. Tell me a story that illustrates a time in your career when you used data to provide information that may have been counter-intuitive or may have led to changes in the way that the organization operated.

23. The Importance of Mentorship

    a. Do you have or have you ever had a mentor? Who was it?

    b. What did you learn from your mentor that has affected you throughout your career?

    c. Tell me a story that illustrates how a mentor affected your career success.

24. Play to Your Strengths

    a. What do you consider to be the one or two major strengths that you have used throughout your career?

    b. Have you ever been in a situation where you hesitated to use your strengths for a particular reason?

    c. Tell me a story that illustrates how you used a key strength to achieve a difficult objective during your career.

25. Sometimes You Have to Do It Yourself

a. During your career, have you ever been part of a team on which communication was less than perfect?

b. If so, what effect did the imperfect communication have on the team's success or failure?

c. Tell me a story that illustrates how you personally overcame less-than-perfect communication on a team or a project. What did you specifically do to ensure its ultimate success, and what did you learn from the experience?

26. Sometimes You Should Trust Your Gut

a. Can you think of a situation during your career where you used a "gut feeling" or intuition instead of logical analysis to make a successful decision?

b. If so, in looking back, were there any factors just below your conscious level that may have helped you reach that decision?

c. Tell me a story that illustrates how you used a "gut feeling" or intuition instead of logical analysis to make a successful decision.

27. Sometimes You Have to Move

    a. Have you ever been in a career situation where you felt underappreciated by your boss or by the organization you worked for?

    b. If so, how did you handle the situation? What techniques did you use to improve the extent to which you were appreciated? If you left, was the "grass greener" on the other side?

    c. Tell me a story that illustrates how you overcame a sense of underappreciation at work during your career.

28. We Should All Get Along (Or Not)

    a. Have you ever been in a situation during your career where you have been unable to get along with another person on the job?

    b. If so, did the communication between the two of you suffer, or were you able to maintain good communication for the good of your organization or project?

    c. Tell me a story that illustrates how either you or someone you know overcame interpersonal differences on the job, and that ultimately led to the success of the organization or of a project.

Lessons Learned

29. Don't Be Mean to an End

 a. Have you ever been terminated by an organization or have you ever had to terminate the employment of another person during your career?

 b. If you were terminated, what feelings did you experience? If you have had to terminate others, what feelings did you experience?

 c. Tell me a story that illustrates how you handled the experience of being fired or how, if you have had to fire another person, you were able to maintain the self-esteem of that person to the greatest extent possible.

30. Humour Is a Very Serious Thing

 a. To what extent do you think that a good sense of humour is important to career success?

 b. What was the funniest one-liner you have come across over the course of your career?

 c. Tell me a story that illustrates how humour helped you or someone else over the course of your career.

31. Fifteen Minutes of Fame

    a.   Have you ever had a brush with fame?

    b.   If so, how long did the experience last and how, if at all, did it change you or the way that others perceived you?

    c.   Tell me a story that illustrates how you or someone you know was affected by a brush with fame during your career.

32. Don't Leave for Money; Don't Stay Out of Fear

    a.   If you have been with your employer for a long time, why have you stayed? Is fear of something new a primary factor in your decision to stay?

    b.   What were your reasons for leaving the employers you left? Was money ever a primary factor in your decision to leave?

    c.   Tell me a story that illustrates how you or someone you know left an organization for the wrong reasons and what you learned from the experience.

33. The Power of Money

a. What does money represent to you? Is it a means of obtaining necessities or material goods, a means of "keeping score," or something else?

b. Has the way you value money changed for you over time?

c. Tell me a story that illustrates how money has influenced your behaviour in either a positive or a negative manner.

34. Find and Keep the Right Partner

a. Have you ever had to make a decision about your career that had a direct impact on another person?

b. If so, what criteria did you use to assess the merits of your career decision?

c. Tell me a story that illustrates how you or someone you know made a career decision that affected a partner and what you learned from the experience.

35. Find Your Reason

    a.   What is the most important aspect of your life? What makes you want to get up in the morning?

    b.   Has your most important thing changed for you over time?

    c.   Tell me a story that illustrates how your "reason for living" keeps you going.

Acknowledgements

As I say in the preface to this book, we are all characters in each other's stories. I am truly grateful to every character in every story throughout my life, whether included in this book or not. Whether we shared positive or negative experiences, you have shaped and continue to shape who I am.

I am especially grateful to those people who inspired me to write down these stories and who provided guidance and advice throughout the process. First to my daughters —Rachelle, Natalie, and Jackie, who provided the spark and whose review of early drafts led to my changing certain phraseology to make my words sound less "dated," shall I say. To my wife and partner, Elaine, who put up with my disappearances while I wrote, as well as my many other foibles during our 30 years together. And to my numerous friends and colleagues for their interest and support.

I specifically would like to thank Jo Ann Phillips, Orgad Gratch, Miki Grosz, and Allison McKay who read early drafts and supplied much needed feedback. And to Zsolt Kekesi, the original F… of the Mountain, whose friendship over the years I value, and whose advice about the manuscript made it take shape. Hup Holland.

Finally to all of Greg`s team at Iguana Books and specifically to Kate Unrau, whose editing of my words was painless (for me) and makes it seem like I know how to write. Thank you.

Iguana Books
iguanabooks.com

If you enjoyed *Lessons Learned*...
Look for other books coming soon from Iguana Books! Subscribe to our blog for updates as they happen.

iguanabooks.com/blog/

You can also learn more about Paul Farkas and his upcoming work on his Iguana Books page.

paulfarkas.iguanabooks.com/

If you're a writer ...
Iguana Books is always looking for great new writers, in every genre. We produce primarily ebooks but, as you can see, we do the occasional print book as well. Visit us at iguanabooks.com to see what Iguana Books has to offer both emerging and established authors.

iguanabooks.com/publishing-with-iguana/

If you're looking for another good book ...
All Iguana Books books are available on our website. We pride ourselves on making sure that every Iguana book is a great read.

iguanabooks.com/bookstore/

Visit our bookstore today and support your favourite author.

www.ingramcontent.com/pod-product-compliance
Lightning Source LLC
Chambersburg PA
CBHW022108090426
42743CB00008B/765